This pathbreaking book provides a way out of the conceptual and policy cul-de-sac on precarious work for young people, that has dominated research and policy formation. Driven by the question 'how did precarious work come to be the "new normal" for young people?', the authors trace changing working conditions in the UK, Denmark and Germany from the mid-1970s. This 'long view' exposes the suffering inflicted on young people by successive government policies and sets a new research and policy framework within which young people's lives can be built.

**Johanna Wyn**, *Director of the Youth Research Centre, Australia*

Some of these authors have been holding the flame for youth studies for the last thirty years. Here, in a new must-read book analysing changes over that time, they show how vulnerable youth should no longer be regarded as a generation 'lost' to the labour market. Instead, they are now a 'liminal' generation in the labour market, caught betwixt and between by precarious employment.

**Chris Warhurst**, *Professor and Director of the Warwick Institute for Employment Research, Warwick University, UK*

An ambitious contribution that will shape how we understand the worlds of work of young people. From YOPs and YTSs in the 1980s to zero-hours contracts in the contemporary post-'great recession' UK marked by youth unemployment, underemployment and economic instability, Furlong et al. unpack the alternatives to long-term full-time employment that have been available to young people. Their empirically-grounded analysis of change, and continuities, in the labour market offers a critical engagement with the influential notion of 'precariat'. They develop instead a new model, with three 'zones of (in)security', to provide a more nuanced theoretical approach to the diverse working lives of young people.

**Tracey Warren**, *Professor of Sociology, School of Sociology and Social Policy, University of Nottingham, UK*

# Young People in the Labour Market

Levels of suffering among young people have always been much higher than governments suggest. Indeed, policies aimed at young workers have often been framed in ways that help secure conformity to a new employment landscape in which traditional securities have been progressively removed. Increasingly punitive welfare regimes have resulted in new hardships, especially among young women and those living in depressed labour markets.

Framed by the ideas of Norbert Elias, *Young People in the Labour Market* challenges the idea that changing economic landscapes have given birth to a 'Precariat' and argues that labour insecurity is more deep-rooted and complex than others have suggested. Focusing on young people and the ways in which their working lives have changed between the 1980s recession and the Great Recession of 2008/2009 and its immediate aftermath, the book begins by drawing attention to trends already emerging in the preceding two decades.

Drawing on data originally collected during the 1980s recession and comparing it to contemporary data drawn from the UK Household Longitudinal Study, the book explores the ways in which young people have adjusted to the changes, arguing that life satisfaction and optimism are linked to labour market conditions.

A timely volume, this book will be of interest to undergraduate and postgraduate students, as well as postdoctoral researchers who are interested in fields such as Sociology, Social Policy, Management and Youth Studies.

**Andy Furlong** was Professor of Social Inclusion and Education and Dean for Research in the College of Social Science at the University of Glasgow, as well as Honorary Professorial Fellow at the University of Melbourne and Conjoint Professor at the University of Newcastle, Australia.

**John Goodwin** is a Professor of Sociology at the University of Leicester.

**Henrietta O'Connor** is a Professor of Sociology at the University of Leicester.

**Sarah Hadfield** is a Researcher at the Institute of Mental Health, Nottingham. She worked as a Researcher at the University of Leicester when this book was formulated.

**Stuart Hall** is a Senior Researcher in the Robert Owen Centre for Educational Change at the University of Glasgow.

**Kevin Lowden** is a Senior Researcher in the Robert Owen Centre for Educational Change at the University of Glasgow.

**Réka Plugor** works as a Researcher at the University of Leicester.

# Youth, Young Adulthood and Society
**Series editor:** Andy Furlong, University of Glasgow, UK

The **Youth, Young Adulthood and Society** series brings together social scientists from many disciplines to present research monographs and collections, seeking to further research into youth in our changing societies around the world today. The books in this series advance the field of youth studies by presenting original, exciting research, with strongly theoretically- and empirically-grounded analysis.

*Published:*

### The Subcultural Imagination
Theory, Research and Reflexivity in Contemporary Youth Cultures
*Edited by Shane Blackman and Michelle Kempson*

### Muslim Youth in the Diaspora
Challenging Extremism through Popular Culture
*Pam Nilan*

### Young People in the Labour Market
Past, Present, Future
*Andy Furlong, John Goodwin, Henrietta O'Connor, Sarah Hadfield, Stuart Hall, Kevin Lowden and Réka Plugor*

*Forthcoming:*

### Youth, Class and Culture
*Steven Threadgold*

### Spaces of Youth
Identities, Inequalities and Social Change
*David Farrugia*

### Rethinking Young People's Marginalisation
Beyond Neo-Liberal Futures?
*Perri Campbell, Lyn Harrison, Chris Hickey and Peter Kelly*

# Young People in the Labour Market

Past, Present, Future

Andy Furlong, John Goodwin, Henrietta O'Connor, Sarah Hadfield, Stuart Hall, Kevin Lowden and Réka Plugor

Routledge
Taylor & Francis Group

LONDON AND NEW YORK

First published 2018
by Routledge
2 Park Square, Milton Park, Abingdon, Oxon OX14 4RN

and by Routledge
711 Third Avenue, New York, NY 10017

*Routledge is an imprint of the Taylor & Francis Group, an informa business*

*British Library Cataloguing in Publication Data*
A catalogue record for this book is available from the British Library

*Library of Congress Cataloging in Publication Data*
A catalog record for this book has been requested

ISBN: 978-1-138-79806-9 (hbk)
ISBN: 978-1-315-75675-2 (ebk)

Typeset in Times New Roman
by Deanta Global Publishing Services, Chennai, India

MIX
Paper from
responsible sources
FSC
www.fsc.org    FSC™ C013985

Printed in the United Kingdom
by Henry Ling Limited

# Contents

# Figures

# Tables

# Preface

## Working with Andy Furlong on *Young People in the Labour Market: Past, Present and Future*

... we have seen that some of the problems faced by young people in modern Britain stem from an attempt to negotiate difficulties on an individual level. Blind to the existence of powerful chains of interdependency, young people frequently attempt to resolve collective problems through individual action and hold themselves responsible for their inevitable failure.

(Furlong and Cartmel 1997: 114)

Andy Furlong was at the forefront of youth studies in the UK and beyond from the late 1980s. He was an intellectual leader for the discipline and someone whose drive and commitment to understanding the problems of youth brought many academic colleagues along with him. At the heart of his research was a grave concern for, as the above quotation suggests, the problems experienced by young people themselves as they made the increasingly complex transitions from education (in all its forms) to employment. It was these problems, and the question of how the powerful chains of interdependency had continued or changed over time, that we envisaged as being central to the arguments developed in this book.

The origins of *Young People in the Labour Market: Past, Present, Future* are based on ideas first aired in 2001, and again in 2006, when we had discussed with Andy the possibility of revisiting legacy data from research projects and themes he had been associated with while he was at the University of Leicester in the 1980s. These ideas were finally crystallised in 2011 when we applied to the Economic and Social Research Council for funding. The aim was to examine what we could (re)learn from 'legacy' datasets in relation to 'past' youth transitions. Also, when combined with contemporary data, what this data could tell us about longer-term change and transformations in youth employment between the 1980s recession and the Great Recession of 2008/2009 and its immediate aftermath. More specifically, by linking past and present data through our research *Making the 'Precariat': Unemployment, Insecurity and Work-Poor Young Adults in Harsh Economic Conditions* we sought to examine how the lives of young people changed between these two important periods of economic instability in the UK. This research lasted for 3 years and, despite the complexities of the data (see main text), together with Andy we felt that there was a clear story to tell, so we began to work on the book. After a slow start writing progressed well, and we were hopeful that the book not only had something important to say but would make a distinctive contribution to the field. By October 2016 we had a full draft and, shortly before the school half-term holiday, we travelled to Glasgow to finalise the draft chapters of this book with Andy. We spent a productive and enjoyable day working through each chapter line by line – with Andy perfecting each sentence (typically), hammering the keyboard as he went. We broke for lunch and spoke of half-term holiday plans with our respective families – Andy characteristically describing how he had work to complete before leaving for Italy the next day. We returned to Leicester, energised and happy that the book was fully drafted and excited about the plans for our latest project focused on the long-term impacts of youth participation in youth training schemes. Of course, we were unaware that this was to be the last of our meetings in person.

Work continued on the book up to Christmas with regular email exchanges, Dropbox updates and conversations about the plans for a book launch event for 2017. Shortly after the full draft was submitted to the publisher, and we had corresponded on the final corrections and proofs, we received the devastating news of Andy's unexpected death. On hearing this news, we initially lost all motivation and interest in continuing with this project or finishing the book. It somehow seemed wrong to do so without Andy leading the way. It was Andy's drive and commitment to the book, and to the research project which preceded it, that kept us moving forward. Despite being over-committed elsewhere, Andy kept us in check and (largely) on track with the writing. In return, it was our commitment to him as a friend (first and foremost) and colleague that maintained our enthusiasm, determination and motivation. So how could we carry on this work without Andy? It would be hard and emotional with a clear feeling that the book was coming to represent something else to us, other than a piece of research. However, in the few months since his death we have had much time to reflect on the work, Andy's other work and his legacy. What emerged was the sense that he would now be telling us to stop being sentimental and to get the book finished – 'Get on with it,' he would email, 'it needs to be finished!' Knowing that this was clearly an important book for Andy and ourselves – as well as the subsequent realisation that this volume has far more significance than any of the team could ever have imagined, since this may well be Andy's final publication – we knew we had a responsibility to Andy to move forward and to complete the work as soon as we could. For us, the book is also important as its core themes encompass Andy's wider body of work in single volume, encapsulated perfectly in the title: *Young People in the Labour Market: Past, Present and Future.*

## Past

We had known Andy personally and professionally since the early 1990s via his associations with our former department, The Centre for Labour Market Studies. Andy had long and deep connections with the University of Leicester. He studied Sociology there, obtained his PhD from Leicester under the supervision of Professor David Ashton, and was also awarded a DLitt by Leicester in 2012. His style of working, as well as his core academic concerns, were evident during this early phase of his work, with his PhD thesis coming to exemplify Andy's subsequent career. As his PhD supervisor notes:

> It was typical of Andy that he succeeded in finishing his PhD well within the three years while also holding down part-time jobs to support his family. His studentship was linked to a Department of Employment financed research project on Young Adults in the Labour Market which examined the labour market experience of the YTS generation. That PhD provided the springboard from which Andy moved forward to create a reputation as one of the leading, if not the leading authority on the transition from school to work, the youth labour market and youth studies, both nationally and internationally.
>
> (David Ashton, 2017)

Andy's PhD was soon followed by a stream of articles and books that firmly established his reputation and set the agenda for over two decades of youth labour market research. It is hard to cover all the key works here, but Andy's notable and influential contributions that have had a clear impact on the field include: *Growing Up in a Classless Society? School to Work Transitions* (1992); *Schooling for Jobs: Changes in the Career Preparation of British School Children* (1993); *Hungary, The Politics of Transition* (1995), co-edited with Terry Cox; *Youth, Citizenship and Social Change in a European Context* (1997), edited with John Bynner and Lynn Chisholm; *Young People and Social Change: Individualisation and Risk in the Age of High Modernity* (1997 and 2007), with Fred Cartmel; *Youth Unemployment in Rural Areas* (2000), with Fred Cartmel; *17 in 2003: Findings from the Scottish School Leavers Survey* (2004), with Biggart *et al.*; *Vulnerable Young Men in Fragile Labour Markets: Employment, Unemployment and the Search for Long-Term Security* (2004) and *Higher Education and Social Justice* (2009), with Fred Cartmel; *Are Cultures of Worklessness Passed Down the Generations?* (2012) with Shildrick and Macdonald *et al.*, as well as many others. The sheer impact of this research is clear and, indeed, one only has to check the bibliography of most papers on youth employment to find at least one, usually more, of these works cited. Of these *Young People and Social Change* (1997) is worthy of special mention here as, for many, it is Andy's seminal text in youth studies. Co-authored by Andy and Fred Cartmel when both were at the University of Glasgow, this is Andy's most highly cited piece of work and it was this volume, above all others, that secured Andy's place as a leading youth studies scholar and which continues to be highly influential in the field. The sub-title of the book is 'individualisation and risk in late modernity', and this encapsulates its importance to our understanding of youth transitions. Here, Andy and Fred focused their attention on social changes that impacted young people's lives, questioning the emerging and established orthodoxies via their often-quoted position 'life in late modernity revolves around an epistemological fallacy: although social structures, such as class, continue to shape life chances, these structures tend to become increasingly obscure as collectivist traditions weaken and individualist values intensify' (Furlong and Cartmel 1997: 2).

Not content with writing and reporting on his own primary research from the field, Andy also edited substantial and influential collections and textbooks, including *Youth Studies: An Introduction* (2012), the *Handbook of Youth and Young Adulthood: New Perspectives and Agendas* (2009), the *Routledge Handbook of Youth and Young Adulthood* (2016) and the *Routledge Handbook of the Sociology of Higher Education* (2016) edited with James E. Côté. For Andy, these edited collections were not merely banal acts of research dissemination but were, instead, essential vehicles for highlighting the vibrancy, scope, breadth, depth and significance of work in the field of youth studies. Editing collections such as these, containing fifty-plus chapters, and the need to liaise with authors constantly, is more than a labour of love; it represents a commitment to the field and the subject matter in hand so that we can all better understand it. Andy wrote in the introduction to his latest handbook:

> the contributing authors are given the opportunity to account for the ways in which modern youth life is played out in a wide range of contexts and to highlight the significant changes in their life experiences. Since the last edition, some of the trends previously identified have accelerated … As such, there is a real need to draw attention to the ways in which young people are making their lives under these new conditions.
>
> (Furlong 2016: 4)

Our understanding of the ways in which modern youth life is played out in these various contexts, and the changing life and opportunity structures for young people, have also been meticulously examined in the *Journal of Youth Studies* (JYS). This journal was founded by Andy in 1998, and through his sheer energy and commitment as Editor-in-Chief of JYS, Andy moved this journal from humble origins to being the leading multidisciplinary and international journal for the field. Through his efforts with JYS 'youth studies' moved front and centre as an academic concern within some social science disciplines, as evidenced by the journal's wide readership and successful biannual conference.

## Present

While we had many future projects, writing plans and ideas planned, this book turned out to be our last 'direct' collaboration with Andy. However, our collaboration will continue for a good while with Andy in absentia. Before his death, and now poignantly, we had received funding from the British Academy for the research *Youth Opportunities? The Long-Term Impacts of Participation in Youth Training Schemes during the 1980s*. This is a project specifically designed to combine the themes of this current book (continuities and change over time, data reuse, legacy data and the power of large-scale datasets to enhance our understanding of wider issues and trends in youth labour markets, and so forth) with themes examined directly by Andy in his PhD and his earlier publications. Andy began writing at a time when youth training schemes (YTS) had become, in the UK at least, a stock response by governments to 'alleviating' youth unemployment and addressing changing skills and training needs in the context of massive labour market change and transformation. However, these schemes were highly problematic and contentious.

> Will the Secretary of State acknowledge that, despite the Government's massive propaganda exercise, the customers of the YTS – the youngsters – do not believe that they will receive that which they most desire, which is full-time permanent employment, at the end of the scheme? Does he further acknowledge that YTS is no longer about providing a permanent bridge between school and work, to use the fine words that were used when the scheme was launched four years ago, but is more a gangway to the dole queue for about one-third of the youngsters, who fail to obtain a job when they complete their scheme?
>
> (Evans 1985: 25)

The concerns of UK Members of Parliament were echoed in Andy's research and, in his 1987 PhD, he argued that 'I would suggest the main short-coming of the YTS in Leicester lies in its failure to attract young people destined for low-skilled jobs, and in its failure to be seen as anything more than second best'(Furlong 1987: 227). Andy returned to these themes in his first monograph *Growing up in Classless Society* (1992), published in 1992 while he was a lecturer in Sociology in the Department of Government at the University of Strathclyde. The book, focused on Scottish school leavers, is a text undergirded with notions of social injustice, social reproduction and the need to document clearly the impact of social class on the youth transitions in the context of high levels of youth unemployment, the increasing role of government employment schemes and a contracting youth labour market. Here his research reinforced the view that 'unemployment schemes are experiences largely reserved for those following disadvantaged routes into the labour market' (Furlong 1992: 152). Or as Kerckhoff (1994: 1692) suggests:

> Furlong believes that YTS served to increase the inequalities already found in the Scottish educational system … Among those in YTS, the most disadvantaged were most often in the kinds of programs that were least likely to lead to employment afterwards. Many employers simply used the program trainees so long as the government was paying the bill but did not keep the trainees on as regular employees afterwards. Furlong argues that such trainees thus became 'double failures'.

What happened to those who participated in the 1980s youth training schemes? What was to become of these 'double failures' Andy had identified? What were the long-term career and life 'impacts' for those who participated in YTS? Were these 'tacky' job substitution schemes or did they (ever) provide gateways to real and meaningful work? More specifically, and together, we aimed to explore the long-term value of government interventions by interviewing participants more than 30 years after they completed schemes. This approach to understanding the impact of YTS on subsequent employment histories was to combine qualitative interviews with 1980s YTS participants, the secondary analysis of 'legacy datasets' on 1980s youth training schemes and via an analysis of the 1970 British Birth Cohort study. It was in this final area that Andy was to lead, given his previous experiences of working with data such as Scottish School Leavers Surveys and the fact that he had used data from the fourth sweep of the 1970 British Birth Cohort in *Schooling for Jobs* (1993). Andy was to revisit this data and to update the 'YTS in the BCS70' story, but mindful of Connolly's (1993: 82) plea that 'qualitative analyses to complement Furlong's work would go a long way in addressing the reasons behind the evidently continued reproduction of existing social inequalities'.

## Future: move forward

There are many themes from Andy's earlier works that are revisited in this book and are perhaps best encapsulated by reference to the opening and closing chapters of this book. David Ashton and Ken Roberts were invited to provide these contributions in recognition of their own considerable influence on the field of youth studies and on the work of Andy over the preceding four decades. Both conclude their contributions expressing hope for young people in the future: that that there will be 'an escape ... from neo-liberalism and a vision of an alternative future' for young people 'based on broader humanitarian values'. These sentiments without doubt chime strongly with Andy's own concerns for the future development of youth policy.

Indeed, his concern for social justice for young people continued to the end, as one of his very rare forays into the world of social media soon after the EU referendum suggested:

@Andy_furlong – Brexit: The wrinklies have well and truly stitched us up

Major changes in the political landscape, such as Brexit or Scottish independence represent yet more 'new conditions', further 'significant changes in their life experiences' and additional 'collective problems', all of which still further compound the problems faced by young people in modern Britain and the difficulties they have to contend with. We feel sure if Andy were here he would now be turning his attention directly to these concerns. Alas not. Andy was a friend, a colleague, a counsellor, an advisor and a good man. Like so many others we will miss him immensely and it remains impossible to imagine the world of youth studies without him being part of it. He was a 'doer', he got things done, and his international reputation stands testimony to that. Andy's legacy will be long-lasting and we must move forward to celebrate his life as the leading scholar in our field in the very best way that we can – by carrying on the work. For ourselves, we are happy to have played a small part in helping Andy achieve what he wanted to achieve with this book. Any errors or omissions that remain are ours and not Andy's.

John Goodwin and Henrietta O'Connor

# Acknowledgements

The authors wish to acknowledge support from the Economic and Social Research Council for the project entitled 'The Making of the Precariat', funded under Phase 1 of the Secondary Data Analysis Initiative (ES/K3755/1). We would also like to acknowledge the Understanding Society team at the University of Essex, the Institute for Social and Economic Research and NatCen Social Research. At Glasgow, Niamh Friel and Hannah Walters both assisted with analysis and reporting.

Our greatest debt is to David Ashton, Emeritus Professor at the University of Leicester, and Ken Roberts, Emeritus Professor at the University of Liverpool. Dave and Ken not only provided us with the opening and closing chapters for this volume, they also provided us with original data they collected in the 1980s and helped us understand some of the context. As colleagues we have worked with in different ways over several decades, they also inspired some of the thinking behind the book. We would also like to acknowledge the research teams who worked on these two projects.

Thanks also to Emily Briggs and Elena Chiu at Routledge for their patience!

> Liberty without protection can give rise to the very worst of servitudes, that of need.
>
> (Castel 2003: 6)

# Authors

**Andy Furlong** was Professor of Social Inclusion and Education and Dean for Research in the College of Social Science at the University of Glasgow, as well as Honorary Professorial Fellow at the University of Melbourne and Conjoint Professor at the University of Newcastle, Australia. Andy was a Fellow of the Academy of Social Science, editor-in-chief of the *Journal of Youth Studies*, and worked with a range of governments and NGOs on youth employment and training-related issues.

**John Goodwin** is a Professor of Sociology at the University of Leicester. As a sociologist, his principal research interests include the broad areas of youth, community and research methods well as the history of sociology. John is a recognised expert on the life and sociology of Pearl Jephcott. He also has a significant interest in the works of Norbert Elias and C. Wright Mills. He has expertise in qualitative secondary analysis, restudies, biographical methods and the use of unconventional data sources in sociological research.

**Henrietta O'Connor** is a Professor of Sociology at the University of Leicester. Her research interests focus on the sociology of work and employment, in particular transitions to and from the labour market. She has published widely on aspects of the transition process, for example, young people's experiences of leaving education and entering work, older people making the transition to retirement and mothers returning to employment. She also has an active interest in research methods with a focus on online methods, the secondary analysis of qualitative data and qualitative longitudinal research.

**Sarah Hadfield** is a Researcher at the Institute of Mental Health, Nottingham. Sarah's research interests fall within Public Policy and Sociology. She has worked on multiple research projects on subjects including the organisation of work, youth (un)employment and transitions. Her current research is on employment insecurity, gender and finances. Sarah is currently conducting both evaluation and academic research and has much experience in qualitative methods, research evaluation, archive research and historical data analysis.

**Stuart Hall** is a Senior Researcher in the Robert Owen Centre for Educational Change at the University of Glasgow. Prior to this he was a Research Officer at the Scottish Council for Educational Research. He has been involved in more than 70 policy-related research or evaluation projects and has undertaken work for organisations including the Scottish government, the European Union and a number of charities. He has a wide range of experience in the use of both quantitative and qualitative research methods and has a particular interest in the use of evaluation for organisational development and improvement.

**Kevin Lowden** is a Senior Researcher in the Robert Owen Centre for Educational Change at the University of Glasgow, with a background in sociology and education. He has almost 30 years' experience as a researcher and principal investigator on national and international research and evaluation projects. Much of his research has focused on assessing the impact of innovative education programmes, with the findings directly informing policy and practice. Over the past decade, his work has had an emphasis on researching and supporting partnership working and collaborative action research to inform educational change.

**Rékar Plugor** works as a Researcher at the University of Leicester. Her background is in sociology and policy studies, and she has a broad range of research interests located mainly within sociology of education, youth and work. She conducts research on these topics from both theoretical and applied perspectives using qualitative, quantitative or mixed methods. Her recent work explores the relationship between higher education and the world of work through the experiences and perceptions of university students in England and Romania.

# Contributions

Andy Furlong, John Goodwin and Henrietta O'Connor were jointly responsible for writing the text and were co-applicants for the ESRC project research *Making the 'Precariat': Unemployment, Insecurity and Work-Poor Young Adults in Harsh Economic Conditions* (Grant number ES/K003755/1). We fully acknowledge and thank the ESRC for the funding to undertake this research.

Stuart Hall and Kevin Lowden were jointly responsible for the secondary analysis of several waves of the *Understanding Society* database. In addition, they contributed to the development of new variables for analysis of the data on young people. They produced a number of summary reports of findings from this exercise which informed the conceptual work of Professor Furlong.

Sarah Hadfield was a research assistant on the project that lead to the book. Sarah's role included conducting re-interviews with the 1980s research team and the preparation of the legacy data for re-use. Sarah contributed to the writing of the methodological appendix and conducted literature searches and primary source findings that were used mainly in Chapters 2 and 3. She also assisted with quality checking and cleaning of the datasets.

Réka Plugor was a researcher on the project whose role included transposing the 1980s datasets into SPSS, quality checking and cleaning the datasets and creating a merged 1980s dataset for the analysis. Réka supported the analysis of the 1980s datasets and produced a number of the charts and tables from the 1980s used in Chapter 3.

# Looking back in order to look forwards

## The 'golden age'

There really was a golden age when smooth and rapid school-to-work transitions were the norm. I left school in that era. This was at age 16 in 1957, when I was offered a job in every bank and insurance company to which I applied. In spring 1961 I quit the bank where I had spent nearly 4 years, having been accepted at university. I wanted an immediate boost in pay. The Monday after leaving my bank, I started work in a factory that manufactured floor tiles. The work was tedious and heavy, as were many jobs at that time, and we worked more hours per day than at the bank. We worked overtime into early evenings and on Saturday mornings whenever it was offered: the extra hours were paid at normal rate plus 50 per cent. But it was tough, so I quit and the following day started work in the despatch department of a confectionery factory. These jobs paid an adult wage irrespective of age, unlike the bank, which had a long incremental salary scale. My pay was 50 per cent higher (without overtime) doing manual jobs. My intellectual interest in the entry into employment began at that time. How was it possible to stick that kind of work for life?

Not everything was golden in those years. There was the 11-plus. This did not consign three-quarters of all children to a scrapheap (there was a genuine alternative route through further education), but it assured those who passed (and, more significant, their parents) that they were safe: they would not face lifetimes in hard, tedious jobs. Very few leavers from grammar schools (such as my own) progressed to university. There was plenty of talent for the 'alternative route' to recruit. Roughly half of grammar school boys left at 16 (or quit earlier at age 15), when most started apprenticeships. Grammar school girls went into office jobs.

There were men's jobs and women's jobs. The Youth Employment Bureaux had separate sections for boys and girls. Adult employment exchanges had men's and women's entrances, registers and jobs. When doing the same jobs, women were usually paid less than men. Race discrimination was normal and blatant prior to Britain's first Race Relations Act in 1965. Homosexuality was illegal until

1967. So was abortion. The contraceptive pill became available from 1961, but its use by young single women did not become normal until the 1970s. The 1950s and 1960s were the decades of 'shotgun weddings'. Young single mothers were told that they 'had' to have their babies adopted. This was the age when youth was described as a 'brief flowering period'.

Today's young people would not choose to recreate the conditions of the 1950s and 1960s even if they were able to do so, but those of us who grew up then did benefit from full employment, and most of us who went to university had our fees paid in full and lived on maintenance grants and vacation jobs. There was net upward social mobility, and even the immobile were able to enjoy superior living standards to their parents. All this was despite some abject policy failures during the post-war reconstruction of Britain. The 1944 Education Act did not lead to 'parity of esteem' between different types of secondary schools. This was the first of successive education policy failures that were supported by the left-leaning educational intelligentsia at that time. It was followed by comprehensive schools, which were introduced without developing a comprehensive curriculum, and unsuccessful attempts to remedy social class inequalities in outcomes through positive discrimination. Even so, young people's education proved an adequate preparation for the labour market. Most of those who were affected could not understand why they were being detained in school until age 15 in 1947 (when the statutory leaving age was raised from 14), and likewise when it was raised to 16 in 1972.

There have been subsequent attempts to label to post-war decades as a dark age when the country was over-burdened with taxes, and when employers were held to ransom by powerful trade union 'barons' and shop stewards. No: it was a high point. At the beginning of this book, these years are presented as the high point of a century-long civilising of employment relations. I see the decades as high points in the achievements of organised labour and its political arm, the Labour Party, aided by the remnants of wartime social solidarity. I refuse to regard this brief episode in our history as a never-to-be-repeated past. Sure, with hindsight, there were mistakes. The nationalised corporation was made a too-dominant model of public ownership. The welfare standards set by Beveridge and his predecessors were so low that in an increasingly affluent society they meant poverty rather than security. The trade unions and their political representatives did not know how to address expanding sections of the workforce: women and white-collar employees. Even so, the decades are a reminder of what remains possible. No one wants to go back. This is impossible. Young people in the 1950s and 1960s knew little about the experiences of predecessors who grew up in the 'hungry 1930s' and had wartime youth experiences. Similarly, young people in the twenty-first century do not compare their circumstances with those who were young 40 or 50 years ago.

Why should they? Most people live in and accept the present, whatever its flaws and merits. However, academics must be able to look back and understand how and why genuine full employment was possible, and how it might be recovered. It never meant jobs for life. Workers could and did move. There were plenty of young job hoppers. Some took breaks. They worked for a bit then did nothing for a while. Neither jobs nor unemployment were considered tolerable for long unbroken periods. It was jobs that had to wait, not job seekers.

The entry into employment was not a problem, and therefore was not a top issue for youth researchers at that time. The hot topics were delinquency (recorded crime had doubled in the 1950s) and the new youth cultures which most adults found both incomprehensible and vaguely threatening. Psychology was the lead discipline in youth studies and had held this position ever since the American psychologist, G. Stanley Hall, discovered adolescence at the beginning of the twentieth century. The standard explanations of delinquency and youth cultures were in terms of raging hormones, changing body shapes and the need to establish an adult identity.

All this changed in the 1970s. Youth and adult unemployment returned. They had not become things of the past. The economists who had taught me at university were wrong on this. Psychology had no explanations. Sociology became the lead discipline in youth studies; the entry into employment became, and has remained, the central youth research issue; and my own career in the research field had a solid base.

## The 1980s

This book's legacy datasets are from the 1980s, but the authors recognise that the trends which were then transforming youth labour markets had begun much earlier. Britain led Europe's post-1945 economic recovery and consolidation of a welfare state; then, although it was not seen like this at the time, Britain began to lead Europe into a post-industrial and neo-liberal age. The immediate cause of the rise in youth (and adult) unemployment in the 1970s was the loss of orders, output and therefore jobs in Britain's manufacturing industries. This trend had been noted in the 1960s. It accelerated in the 1970s, when quadrupled oil prices sent shock waves throughout the global economy. This was a shock from which Britain's economy was expected to recover, and throughout the 1970s youth (and adult) unemployment were treated as a temporary problem which required special measures of finite duration, after which normality would return to the economy and labour markets.

The 1970s is Britain's decade with no historical legacy. In the post-war decades, Britain (and other Western countries) created social democracies. The 1980s saw the dawn of the ongoing neo-liberal age. Apart from punk, the 1970s can be recalled only as the decade when monetary inflation reached record twentieth-century levels (it peaked at 26 per cent), when more days were lost to strikes than at any time since then or in the 1950s and 1960s, and when governments led by both major political parties struggled, ultimately unsuccessfully, to reach agreements with employers and trade unions to control rates of increase in wages and prices. Everything changed in the 1980s. Unemployment (which rose to new record heights) and monetarist policies (limiting the cash that was available for consumers and businesses to spend) brought inflation under control and, along with new industrial relations laws, sapped the power of organised labour.

This treatment of youth unemployment as a temporary problem changed in the 1980s. It was accepted that the former normality had gone for ever. Deindustrialisation (the new term for the decline of manufacturing) accelerated again. Unemployment rose to new post-war record levels. The pace of change was due to the government's monetarist (what would now be called austerity) policies, and the deregulation of markets, which meant allowing 'lame ducks' to sink. The casualties included major steel plants, car assembly factories and, eventually, most of the country's coal mines. It was accepted that the economy and labour markets were being permanently restructured. This led to the divisions of youth labour markets, identified in this volume (though not seen so clearly by researchers such as myself at that time), into traditional, full-time permanent jobs, a heavily constrained (basically unemployed) sector and an in-between zone of liminality. Showing that these three labour market sectors have persisted to the present day is the book's most startling finding. This appears to be the new macro-opportunity structure that awaits Britain's beginning workers. The persistence of these divisions is despite all the intervening changes in education and the economy. Looking back, it is particularly noteworthy that in the relatively buoyant local youth labour markets in the 1980s, unemployment was being contained mainly by the creation of 'liminal' positions rather than traditional, full-time permanent jobs.

More was changing in the 1980s than is evident in the legacy datasets. By the end of the 1980s, deindustrialisation had ceased to be the main trend that was responsible for all the restructuring. The use of new information and communication technologies (ICTs) was spreading throughout the economy. Major service sectors (banks for example), as well as the remaining manufacturing industries, began replacing labour with these new technologies. Also, labour and all other markets were deregulated during the 1980s. Labour markets were deregulated by disempowering trade unions and abolishing the Wages Councils that had set minimum rates in low-paid, weakly unionised industries such as agriculture and retail. Capital was deregulated and allowed to flow freely into and out of the country. Financial businesses were deregulated in one 'big bang' in 1986. It took many years for the effects of these changes to become fully apparent. A short-term outcome was that new 'masters of the universe' working in the City of London's financial services began receiving spectacularly high salaries and bonuses. Meanwhile, the UK workforce was growing, due partly to natural increase but mainly due to increased labour force participation by women, and immigration. There is little chance of closing the door. If workers are not allowed to enter higher-wage countries, the jobs can be offshored.

The 1980s brought a series of new education and training initiatives. These were led by employers, not a left-leaning intelligentsia. All the new initiatives failed. The Youth Opportunities Programme, then successive versions of Youth Training, turned out to be dead ends rather than stepping stones for too many entrants. Economists who advocated labour market deregulation were allowed to experiment. From 1982, the government began subsidising employers who reduced youth rates of pay. Youth unemployment was supposedly due to young people's exorbitant wage expectations. Wages were encouraged to drift down to the level at which the labour markets would clear. Young people with little or no occupational experience were assisted in starting their own businesses. This was supposed to promote the spread of an enterprise culture. Most of the start-ups flopped. However, in the twenty-first century, 'survival self-employment' has continued to be a growth sector, and real wages beneath the middle have continued to decline. Another policy failure was the launch of National Vocational Qualifications (NVQs) in the mid-1980s. Operating alongside the Youth Training Scheme, these new qualifications were supposed to create a firm base for a new alternative vocational route into employment. Their reception in industry was made clear to me at the end of the 1980s, when an employer explained that NVQ stood for 'not very qualified'.

## The 1990s and 2000s

The 1980s was the decade of schemes, but these new routes were never genuinely accepted by young people. They could distinguish between good and bad schemes – those where training was by an employer with the prospect of a permanent job to follow, and those that were dead ends or slave labour – but schemes were never normalised, accepted as a useful first step into the workforce. The step might be accepted as unavoidable by an individual, but he or she could see that others were making transitions straight into proper jobs, probably, and increasingly so over time, after a period in extended, post-compulsory education. Government-supported training schemes are still operating today, but young people often need to be coerced on board by the threat of punitive sanctions (the withdrawal of unemployment benefit). There have always been more appealing routes towards employment. The legacy datasets show that throughout the 1980s many young people (how many depended on where they lived) continued to make traditional one-step transitions into proper jobs at age 16–18. Those who were staying in education beyond age 16 were often doing part-time jobs in which they could earn as much as the Youth Training allowance.

During the 1980s, economists joined sociologists in investigating young people's new routes towards employment. The economists' interest was in returns on investments in human capital measured in chances of avoiding unemployment and earnings when in jobs. A consistent finding was that qualifications earned in education were a better bet than government-supported training schemes. Young people were reading labour market signals correctly when they regarded schemes as a last resort. The economists also found that academic qualifications yielded superior returns to vocational qualifications. Again, young people appear to have read labour market signals correctly. Throughout the 1970s and 1980s comprehensive secondary schools were steadily increasing the proportions of young people passing General Certificate of Education (GCE) O levels then progressing to A levels. The numbers leapt from 1988 onwards, when GCE O levels were merged with Certificates of Secondary Education (CSEs). Then, at the beginning of the 1990s, there was a rapid expansion in the number of students progressing into higher education. This was followed by a steady rise throughout the rest of the 1990s and into the 2000s, so that today roughly half of each cohort has enrolled on a 'tertiary' course by age 30. In the 1990s, governments ceased promoting vocational qualifications (typically Business and Technology Education Council [BTEC] qualifications and then the General NVQs that became available from 1990) as an alternative routes to different careers and began claiming that they were the equivalents of academic qualifications, accepted for university entrance.

As well as learning to use new words such as deindustrialisation and globalisation and acronyms such as ICT, in the 1980s we were also told about the virtues of flexible firms and labour markets, and about a soon-to-arrive knowledge economy. The latest technologies were to eliminate swaths of routine jobs while an unlimited number of high-level, high-value-added, high-salary jobs would be available for all young people who were suitably qualified. The expansion of employment at management and professional levels that had been underway throughout the twentieth century was to accelerate. Advanced economies would do the world's brain work because their advanced education systems would produce the world's best-qualified workforces. How wrong can you be? Britain's school leavers in the 1980s were the last cohort to enter labour markets in which the proportion of jobs at management and professional levels was increasing. During the 1990s, 'emerging market economies' began to outperform the West in producing university graduates. Yet, into the twenty-first century, UK governments continued encouraging young people to invest in their human capital by enrolling in higher education. Former polytechnics and colleges of higher education were upgraded to universities. Much of the old 'alternative route' through further education was absorbed into a new mass higher education system. Today's graduates know the outcomes. Student maintenance grants have been replaced by loans. Maintenance loans are accompanied by fee loans. The UK government pays the ludicrously high rate of £9,000 per student per year in a mass university system. Students are encouraged to incur debts that they will never repay. Many graduates now struggle in the 'zone of liminality' before starting careers in jobs which once required just GCE O levels. Graduates in better-paid jobs find themselves being charged more in interest per month than they repay. They face 30 years in which they will pay a super-tax of 9 per cent on all earnings in excess of £21,000.

However, there is now a genuine, attractive alternative. Some employers have discovered that they can attract 18- and 19-year-olds with top A levels onto apprenticeships in which they will be trained in work situations, gain degrees through part-time study or sandwich years and join graduate career tracks in their early twenties with no debt. The problem is that, as in the 1950s, there are far too few of these higher-level apprenticeships to satisfy demand.

## Looking forward

The main lesson I learn from looking back is that I did not foresee any of the last 50 years. So, all forward looking has to be tentative. The top probability is that change will continue. Britain is part of an inherently unstable global market economy. There could be an expansion of the 'sharing economy' – more Ubers. A citizens' wage is possible, but less likely. There seems sure to be more government initiatives in youth education and training, and more projects for researchers to seek outcomes.

We are now deep into a neo-liberal era. This began in Britain when full employment ceased to be a top priority in economic policy. It was initially displaced by control of the money supply in order to suppress inflation, accompanied by progressive deregulation of all markets which were allowed to set levels of employment (and therefore non-employment). Since the 2007–9 financial crisis, reducing government deficits has become another priority throughout the European Union.

Labour market conditions are actually worse than in Britain for young people throughout most of Europe, not to mention North Africa and the Middle East. Britain has been rather good at creating 'liminal' jobs – self-employed drivers, cleaners, gardeners and so on, plus jobs in hotels, restaurants and other consumer services. Young people must now continue in full-time learning (attending school or college in practice) until age 18. Higher education participation could edge upwards towards 75 per cent. Universities have a financial incentive to recruit. Students may or may not believe that they are investing in their human capital and that this will pay off for them eventually, but for many the appeal is that they see no better immediate alternative to 3 years of student lifestyle. They may regard a degree as the minimum necessary to compete seriously for any full-time job of indefinite duration. Extended liminality in which they taste different jobs prior to settling down may also be normalised.

Youth researchers know, but young adults may still be unaware, that collectively they will fail to match their parents' achievements. Age-for-age they are earning less, and they occupy inferior housing. Today's young people will eventually face retirement on inferior pensions, which many will supplement with another extended period of employment in the liminal zone as their working lives stutter to a close. Our politicians and business leaders keep telling us that we have a strong economy, and these leaders may continue to define those who are struggling as the problem. Many voters still appear to find these messages credible.

There are winners. The proportion of GDP accounted for by wages and salaries has been declining since the 1980s. Top incomes have rocketed further upwards. Graduates from 'top universities' have the best chances of stepping directly onto career ladders that could lead to these dizzy heights. They feel underpaid when earning 'only' twice or three times the average salary. More people own more than one dwelling. More households are renting. Landlordism has returned to Britain. The country is producing more higher education graduates per capita than any other European country and more school leavers who are deficient in basic skills (around a fifth lack basic numeracy and literacy). Books that draw attention to these neo-liberal realities occasionally become bestsellers. This sparks bouts of media indignation. Meanwhile, most young people and their families continue doing the best they can for themselves under ongoing conditions.

This era will not last for ever. We have not reached the end of history, but at present it is impossible to foresee how and when the end will come. We need ideas with which to build a new political generation. We need an escape plan from neo-liberalism and a vision of an alternative future, hopefully one which returns full employment to the top of the economic policy agenda. This will squeeze the heavily constrained and liminal zones in Britain's labour markets for job seekers of all ages, and empty what are really expensive waiting rooms, currently designated as education and training.

Ken Roberts
University of Liverpool

# Chapter 1

# Understanding the changing youth labour market

> The first lesson of modern sociology is that the individual cannot understand his own experience or gauge his own fate without locating himself within the trends of his epoch and the life-chances of all the individuals of his social layer.
>
> (C. Wright Mills 1951: xx)

## Introduction

In this book, our primary interest is in the lives of young people and the ways in which their working lives have changed between the 1980s recession and the Great Recession of 2008–9 and its immediate aftermath, although we begin by drawing attention to trends already emerging in the preceding two decades. Our core concern relates to the suffering inflicted on our younger citizens through the various 'civilising offences' (Elias 1994) committed by governments from the mid-1970s onwards. Looking to the future, the book also offers a glimpse of what the future holds for young workers, especially those who lack resources or who occupy vulnerable positions.

Our aims are achieved through re-analysis of two datasets collected during the 1980s recession (referred to as the historical or legacy datasets), and data collected between 2009 and 2011 as part of the UK Household Longitudinal Study, known as *Understanding Society* (University of Essex 2014). These datasets and materials are described in more detail in the Appendix; however, in summary, they were examined as part of our research project *The Making of the 'Precariat': Unemployment, Insecurity and Work-Poor Young Adults in Harsh Economic Conditions*, which was funded by the UK Economic and Social Research Council under Phase 1 of the Secondary Data Analysis Initiative.

Through this research, we set out to explore unemployment, insecurity and work-poor young adults in harsh economic conditions in the United Kingdom using contemporary and historical/legacy data. Specifically, we wanted to discover in what ways the experiences of unemployed, insecure and vulnerable 18- to 25-year-olds had changed between two key periods of economic instability in the United Kingdom. In relation to this, we also aimed to map the nature and extent of marginality and of precarious or fragmented forms of work in the 1980s and in the contemporary era so as to develop a new understanding of the ways in which positive and negative outcomes occur and are influenced by policy interventions.

In this introductory chapter, we aim to outline the conceptual starting points that have helped us understand the changing nature of the youth labour markets and which inform some of the analysis offered in subsequent chapters.

## Analytical starting points and assumptions

### Analytical 'retreat', sociogenesis and long-term social processes

Precarity, precarious employment and rise of 'the precariat' as a 'new dangerous class' (Standing 2011) have come to dominate recent discourses on and around employment in general and relating to youth employment more specifically. Indeed, the idea of the precariat and the desire to understand trends in precarious working formed the basis for a research project undertaken by the authors. In our research project, *The Making of the 'Precariat'*, we purposefully used both contemporary and historic/legacy data to explore this question. These long-term processes of change and transformation are ones that come into sharp focus when we study the changing experiences of young people. Starting from a hunch that precarious working and, in particular, the precarious nature of youth employment was perhaps not so much a 'contemporary' phenomenon but, instead, was part of a longer-term process of change and transformation in the way we work, we had some initial reservations about Standing's thesis.

In adopting a longer-term analytic approach, we draw inspiration from the sociological practice of Norbert Elias and his model of analysing society in long-term perspective. As Goodwin and Hughes (2011) explain, Elias's sociological approach is underpinned by the three core 'kinds' of question:

- an orientation towards sociogenetic questions, for example, how did 'this' come to be?
- an orientation towards relational questions, for example, in what ways are 'these' interrelated? and
- an orientation towards *Homines aperti*, for example, what broader chains of interdependence are involved in 'this'?

(Goodwin and Hughes 2011: 682; see also Baur and Ernst 2011).

For Elias, sociogenesis is the long-term processes of development and transformation in social relations which go hand in hand with what he termed psychogenesis, or the processes of development and transformation in the psychology, personality or habitus that accompany such social changes. To answer a sociogenetic question, such as 'how did it come to be that precarious working is the new "normality" for youth and other groups?', requires an analysis of the changing balances of power and shifting human interdependencies in relation to work and employment over a long period of time.

> Long-term syntheses, even if only to provide a rough outline, are by no means limited to shedding more light on the problems of past societies only. They also help to create a greater awareness of contemporary problems and especially of potential futures.
>
> (Elias 2006: 407)

However, a review of existing analyses of precarity or the 'the precariat' reveals something of a tendency to focus on the 'contemporary' experiences of work and employment, often with a specific focus on the period following the Great Recession. While in and of themselves there is nothing inherently wrong with such approaches or analyses, as Wright Mills (1951) suggests, limiting the analytical horizon to the present can be problematic: there is a danger of implying that 'the present' or 'the contemporary' are somehow separate from 'the past' and that the two are not linked or do not overlap. The idea that the past is somehow 'hermetically sealed' from the present and that our current experiences of work and employment are not informed by change and transformation over the long term is both epistemologically fallacious and ontologically problematic (see Furlong and Cartmel 1997: 144). This is something particularly relevant in the context of youth studies, which, as a subject matter, almost lends itself to a prioritisation of 'contemporary' issues at the expense of all else.

Such an approach implies that the 'here and now', or the issues of contemporary youth, are wholly different from what went before or simply emerged out of nowhere. For example, one of the most influential and agenda-setting examinations of the precariat is offered by Guy Standing (2011), and, while Standing acknowledges the importance of the emergence of globalisation in the 1970s and earlier labour market transformations, he primarily focuses his analysis on the period immediately before and during the economic crisis of 2008 onwards. He suggests that the numbers entering the precariat accelerate after 2008 and that a new dangerous class can be seen to emerge. Yet, narrowing an analysis to a largely contemporary timeframe ignores what has gone before and prompts us to ask additional questions. For example, what is the evidence for the 'precariat' having existed well before the economic crash of the mid 2000s? Are the economic conditions post 2008 *so* unique that current cohorts of young people share no common experiences with those young people entering work in the 1950s, 1960s, 1970s or 1980s? Is work and employment *more* precarious now than it was is the dark ages, the middle ages or the Victorian and colonial era? Are there no continuities between the past and the present?

For Elias (1987), over-focusing on the 'present' and the restricting of analyses to the 'contemporary' is a problem that he describes as the 'retreat of the sociologists into the present'. Elias strongly critiqued this 'narrowing' of the researcher's attention to immediate problems with a view to solving short-term issues at the expense of understanding their genesis over time. He writes,

> the immediate present into which sociologists are retreating … constitutes just one momentary phase within the vast stream of humanity's development, which, coming from the past, debouches into the present and thrusts ahead possible futures.
>
> (Elias 1987: 223–4)

If we are to truly understand precarity, then a longer-term perspective is needed.

There are a number of implications of such an approach for analysing and understanding precarious working. First, that for the analysis to be complete, and for our understanding to be as full as possible, a longer-term perspective is essential. In short, precarious working and the marginalised labour market positions that young people occupy do not simply emerge in isolation from what has gone before or within a historical vacuum. Rather, forms of employment are the consequences of long-term processes of change and transformation.

Second, precarity itself is not fixed, nor are the dominate modes of work and employment at any one time. Indeed, patterns of employment will continue to change, transform and reconfigure as we move into the future. How people experience work and employment in the future is linked to the experiences of work and employment both now and in the past – a long-term chain of interrelationships that continually evolve and change. Focusing on the contemporary is the equivalent of taking a photograph, a snapshot in time, rather than watching a 'movie' of connected images (see Dunning and Hughes 2013). We cannot 'ignore the fact that every present society has grown out of earlier societies and points beyond itself to a diversity of possible futures' (Elias 1985: 226).

Third, as Elias also suggests, the retreat to the present, especially for disciplines such as sociology, is often driven by a desire for immediate policy decisions. Research is positioned to provide the contemporary evidential base for intervention by the state or state actors. Yet, without understanding the genesis of an issue, such policy interventions are inevitably short term, limited in their impact and (more often than not) doomed to replicate the mistakes of previous policy interventions. In relation to youth employment, one only has to consider the multitude of government-sponsored training programmes implemented from the late 1970s onwards, all of which massage employment rates but do little to address the underlying trends and labour market changes.

There are further problematic assumptions which underpin some of the existing work on precarity – in particular, that 'precariousness' is implicitly measured against an assumed 'gold standard' of full-time, permanent employment. The assumption is that permanent, full-time work is the mode of working that all *should* aspire to and which *should* be on offer to all. It is an assumption that harks back to the 1950s and 1960s as representing something of a 'golden age' of high-quality education, training and employment for young people but which does little to acknowledge that a different employment 'normality' or 'reality' may now exist for young people. Having no direct experience of a society built on full employment that is both permanent and full-time, having no first-hand understanding of this beyond what young people are told by teachers, careers advisors, schools and universities, how young people experience or perceive work and employment may not relate directly to the officially sanctioned discourse of full-time, permanent, paid employment.

A good illustration of this is the use of the metaphor 'lost generation'. This idea, the notion of a generation lost (discussed further in Chapter 3), has been liberally sprinkled through the discussions of precarious working and youth marginalisation (see, for example, Nilsen and Brannen 2014) and political discourse. For example, Nilsen and Brannen (2014) outline how the term is used by youth researchers to describe young people 'out of work', or MacDonald and Marsh (2001) have used 'lost generation' to describe those young people who are identified as 'inactive' or welfare dependent. More recently, MacDonald (2011) extends the 'lost generation' metaphor to graduates entering the labour market but who fail to secure employment. However, few actually question the assumption underpinning this metaphor or consider 'lost from what?' What such analyses point to is youth 'lost' from participation in full-time paid employment or a 'job for life', without acknowledging the attendant labour market transformations and new employment realities. The metaphor 'lost generation' as used in some discussions also appears to have a static permanency attached to it, as though the labour market positions of young people can never and will never change. The idea that groups are 'lost forever' is problematic. Elias also, perhaps, helps us understand why precarious youth employment is set against an assumed 'gold standard' of full-time, permanent employment in some analyses. Elias suggests that

> Adult investigators are apt to investigate either their own problems with regard to young people or, more generally, the problems which adults experience so far as the younger generation is concerned, not problems which confront, and which are experienced by the young generation itself.
>
> (Elias 1962: 1)

In short, not having full-time paid employment could be perceived by 'adult investigators' to be a problem, whereas it may not necessarily be perceived or experienced negatively by young people themselves. Moreover, the analysis should have more reality congruence and not focus on 'what should be' but instead explore and document in more detail 'what is'. What is the experience of precarious work, and what are the longer-term changes and continuities which underpin those experiences?

### Civilising offensives

As we have outlined already, Elias was concerned with long-term processes in the development of human societies, which he called 'civilising processes' (Mennell 2015: 1). Focusing on both sociogenetic and psychogenetic changes via the analysis of historical documents, past texts and, most famously, manners books, Elias was able to explore, sociologically, the transformations of societies, changes in behavioural standards, the formation of states and the control of the means of violence, among other things. For example, in *On the Process of Civilisation* (1939), Elias documents how court societies and 'courtiers' in Europe

> were the product of centuries-long conflicts between many rival warlords, out of which there gradually emerged a smaller number of central rulers, kings who gradually undertook the 'taming of warriors' as the key element in the internal pacification of their lands, a central component of state formation processes.
>
> (Mennell 2006: 429)

These long-term 'civilising processes' are central to understanding how societies and behavioural standards 'came to be' and how societies change and transform. Power is crucial here. Control of the means of violence, whether real or symbolic, gives the holder of the control a significant power advantage to intervene to maintain or even change accepted behavioural standards of that time. Since the industrial revolution, in many countries there has been an accepted habitus of work, an accepted hegemony that individuals who themselves have limited access to resources and power will engage in paid employment for those who have or control power and resources. It is easy to find examples through history where behaviours around paid employment are controlled, such as the loud ringing of a bell at the factory to ensure that those in surrounding villages arrived at work on time for their shifts, through to entire state-based social welfare systems and practices being predicated on an individual's 'fitness to work'.

However, following Mennell (2015: 1), and others, it becomes important to distinguish between 'civilising processes' 'as long-term, intergenerational, unplanned and unintended processes, involving changes in the balance of the typical social habitus', on the one hand, and 'civilising offensives', which are 'in contrast planned, organised and intended' (Mennell 2015: 1), on the other. For example, in relation to civilising processes, Elias (2010: 52) suggests that 'our standard of behaviour and our psychological make-up, was certainly not intended by individual people. And it is this way that human society moves forward as a whole; in this way, the whole of human history has run its course'.

In contrast, civilising offensives are *deliberate* and *premeditated* acts or interventions especially designed to purposely 'improve' or change the behaviours of the 'lower orders, the colonised peoples, and so on – the "outsiders" to the respectable "establishments"' (Mennell 2015: 2). As we have already suggested, in many societies since the industrial revolution an officially sanctioned discourse around the normality of full-time paid employment has been sustained (see Wight 1993). It is an expectation that those who are able to work should work in paid employment for a set number of hours per week. Those who do not engage in paid employment, save for those who are deemed to be legitimately engaged in other roles such as parenthood or who are defined as not needed to work (children, the elderly and so forth), are categorised as 'the outsiders', 'the underclass', the 'chavs', the 'feckless and workless', as 'spongers' 'lazy' or 'welfare dependent'. Indeed, there is an entire discourse which reinforces the primacy of full-time paid employment and which defines those who do not work negatively. It is in relation to this that the idea of civilising offensives becomes particularly powerful.

Throughout the last century or so, there are many examples of deliberate and premeditated acts by the state to ensure that individuals work in ways deemed to be acceptable. For example, in their analysis of employability civilising offensives since the late 1970s, Crisp and Powell (2016) demonstrate how government policies in the United Kingdom were underpinned by three trends:

> a near exclusive focus on addressing youth unemployment through supply-side interventions to improve employability; growing levels of conditionality to enforce attachment to the labour market; and differential treatment of young people relative to other age cohorts. Nearly every single major initiative is premised upon the 'supply-side orthodoxy' that interventions to tackle 'worklessness' should largely focus on improving employability through individual behavioural change by raising the skills, aspirations and work-readiness of young people out of work.
>
> (Crisp and Powell 2016: 7–12)

As Crisp and Powell (2016) also highlight, the key idea here is initiatives by the state, through policy interventions, to transform individual behaviours to ensure compliance with the socially accepted hegemony around paid employment.

## Liminality

There is a long history of labelling those who do not engage in socially approved versions of paid employment as outsiders; as somehow deviant or at odds with dominant norms. However, as we have also argued, labour market transformations and associated industrial decline have meant that the opportunities for young people, or working-age people in general, to work in full-time paid employment throughout their lives have been reduced. The 'gold standard' of full-time paid employment has been replaced with a variety of 'alternative' forms of employment that are precarious, temporary and so forth. Given that industrial societies seem to retain the idea of full-time paid employment as something that all should aspire to, this suggests that the role of those working in such 'alternative' forms of employment is somewhat ambiguous and ill-defined. For example, the very notion of temporary employment is underpinned by ambiguity. The temporary worker is not permanent, does not 'belong' and has no definite occupational identity or career, and his or her future is doubtful, uncertain and risky. It is here that, perhaps, other concepts may help us understand more fully how it came to be that insecure work forms are the new 'normality' for young people – in particular, Elias's assertion that the social role of young people is ambiguous and the idea of 'liminality'.

First, the ambiguous and ill-defined nature of alternative and precarious forms of work dovetails somewhat with the ill-defined and ambiguous social role of young people themselves. In our previous work (Goodwin and O'Connor 2015), we highlighted Elias's assertion that the social role of young people is ambiguous, especially during transitional periods in the life course when their roles lack clarity. At school, at college or within the family, a power ratio has emerged which frames the young persons' position as subordinate to the adults around them. Yet, when they begin to enter work,

> [it] places young workers into a different position not only in relation to parents or to friends, but in relation to adults who are strangers – adult workers, supervisors, managers etc. on whom they depend ... The norms, the behaviour and attitudes of the adults with which they now come into contact often differ considerably from those with which they are familiar in their own family circle or from their contact with masters at school.
>
> (Elias 1961: 1)

The more complex a society, the more complex this process of transition to adulthood or the learning of adult norms becomes. This complexity, for Elias, meant that the transition from childhood to adulthood, from school to work is an 'anxiety arousing transition', as the young person's social existence and social order are threatened. The ill-defined social role of youth and the anxieties caused by the transition to work are compounded by the fact that entering work and becoming an adult, in many respects, has become a 'passage without rites'.

> [their position] is, of course, not determined or chosen by the younger genera-
> tion itself. They are determined by the conditions of industrial societies such
> as ours in the mid twentieth century, i.e. at a specific state of social develop-
> ment. To illustrate this point in the most general way one need only remem-
> ber the fact that today the 'passage towards adult roles' is a 'passage without
> rites'. But even in European societies that has not always been the case; the
> passage to adulthood has not always been regarded as an entirely private and
> personal problem of the individual.
>
> (Elias 1962: 1)

In extending this analysis, Elias (1962) goes on to argue that in the past there were ceremonies and rituals, such as those associated with craft guilds when appren-tices produced their 'masterpiece', and these rituals marked the transition from one social role to another. For Elias, the role of such rituals was to help those mak-ing the transition to work and adulthood to confront fears and anxieties associated with transitioning into the 'unknown'.

Second, Elias's writings on adjustments to adulthood, and the 'passage without rites', link directly to some of the writings around 'liminality'. As others have highlighted, liminality has its origins within the work on rituals by Van Gennep (1909/1977) and latterly developed by Turner (1969), as well as being linked to the work of Douglas (1966) (see, for example, Boland and Griffin 2015; Lopez-Aguado 2012; Jones 2014). For Turner (1969), liminality, or 'liminal individuals', are 'neither here nor there; they are betwixt and between the positions assigned and arrayed by law, custom, convention, and ceremony' (1969: 95), while for Douglas (1966), 'liminal individuals' have 'no status, insignia, secular clothing, rank, kinship position, nothing to demarcate them structurally from their fellows' (1966: 36). The use of liminality in their work relates directly to social sanctioned rituals and rites of passage that individuals pass through as a transformatory pro-cess of 'becoming', suggesting that these 'liminal individuals' remain socially ambiguous and ill-defined (neither one thing or another).

The ritual was an important 'marker' of becoming, and for Van Gennep (1909/1977) there were three phases of rites through which individuals passed – separation (séparation), transition (marge) and incorporation (agrégation). This entails a separation from what was before, a previous role, position or status, through a transition (often marked by a ritual performance, examination, trial or test) on to incorporation into a new role or status. Turner (1974) refines his approach and, alongside liminal individuals and outsiders (or outsiderhood), he considers 'marginals' to be those 'who are simultaneously members of two or more groups whose social definitions and cultural norms are distinct from, and often even opposed to, one another' (La Shure 2005: 233). Turner (1974) suggests that 'marginals like liminars are also bewixt and between, but unlike ritual liminars they have no cultural assurance of a final stable resolution of their ambiguity'.

In many respects, Lave and Wenger's concepts of 'legitimate peripheral participation' and 'community of practice' (Lave and Wenger 1991; Wenger 1998) also have echoes of Van Gennep's (1909/1977) approach – 'legitimate peripheral participation' as a transformatory process of 'becoming' via moving from the 'periphery' to the 'established' though active social participation as learning (see Goodwin 2007 in Hughes *et al.* 2007). As Goodwin (2007) suggests, in Lave and Wenger's approach legitimate peripheral participants do not perceive their peripherality before they enter the workplace but only begin to understand their 'separateness' from the 'established' workers around them when they start to make the adjustment to work and adulthood. It is the ambiguous status that is key here. Likewise, Boland and Griffin's (2015) use of liminality is particularly instructive here. They use liminality to explore job-seeking in welfare policy, arguing that 'unemployment/job-seeking is not simply an economic experience … more speculatively we suggest that unemployment/job-seeking is liminal, though less a meaningful rite of passage or a joyful carnival, but a tedious limbo punctuated by frantic job-seeking' (Boland and Griffin 2015: 30).

Liminality helps us understand that it is hard for young people to now complete the transition for work to adulthood – to pass through Van Gennep's séparation, marge, aggregation successfully. This is because the employment they enter is *characteristically liminal* – precarious work is neither unemployment nor full-time career oriented work as had been traditionally understood but hovers somewhere between. It is a form of work that is neither one thing nor another. By entering such work, it becomes harder for the young to be incorporated into established notions of paid employment, to become workers and fully adult. So, young people in the adjustment to adulthood are also in a kind of limbo. They are no longer children, nor are they yet fully adults. Young people are perhaps the most obvious 'liminal individuals' in the most liminal work roles.

## Towards a 'sociogenesis' of precarious working

Following Elias (2006), we can only provide a rough outline of a long-term syntheses of youth employment, but in so doing we are able to highlight those key events that link the broader social processes with the life-chances and experiences of individuals. Indeed, over the last half decade there have been momentous changes in the world of work. Employment in the once dominant manufacturing industries declined sharply from the late 1960s and, in the United

Kingdom today, employs less than one in ten of the workforce (Comfort 2012). Back in the 1970s, fewer women were employed, and many of those that were held part-time jobs. A programme of privatisation has significantly reduced the number of workers employed in the public sector, and final salary pension schemes, which were once relatively common among salaried workers in the public sector, have largely been abandoned in favour of less generous pension schemes where returns are subject to the unpredictability of the market. Trade union membership has fallen sharply, partly due to the decrease in employment in the manufacturing industries, but also due to privatisation and to increased employment in small-scale service units.

There have also been important changes in employment practice, including a fall in the numbers employed on full-time ongoing contacts, underpinned by moves to weaken the legislation that once helped secure tenure and protect workers from unfair or arbitrary dismissal. New contractual arrangements have been introduced, such as zero hours contracts where an employer makes no guarantee about the number of working hours (or the pay) offered, while agency work and temporary work contracts have become more common. Welfare entitlements for those without work have been reduced, and conditions under which support may be claimed have become harsher. Poor wages also mean that many working households in the United Kingdom depend on benefits in order to achieve a minimum standard of living. Indeed, the majority of those classed as being in poverty (having an income of less than 60 per cent of the national median) live in families where at least one of the members is in employment (MacInnes *et al.* 2013).

Of course, levels of employment are always in flux: there was a recession in the mid-1970s linked to the 1973 oil crisis, followed by recessions in the early 1980s and early 1990s. The most recent recession, occurring in 2008–9, was triggered by the fallout from the bursting of the housing bubble in the United States and the ensuing failure of several large banks. This recession, frequently referred to as the 'Great Recession', or the Global Financial Crisis, was the most severe since the 1930s 'Great Depression' (Reuters 2012).

In recessions, a slowdown in economic activity triggers a fall in investment and an increase in unemployment; and unemployment may continue to rise for some time after the recession is officially over. Furthermore, recessions encourage employers to look for cost savings, with the most common responses being pay freezes, a reduction in paid overtime and the implementation of more flexible employment practices such as an increased use of agency workers and fixed term contracts (CBI 2009). Revised employment practices which cut costs and increase profitability may become standard practice after a recession. As such, recessions can be linked to longer-term changes in employment conditions. Recessions may also mark a watershed in a country's industrial profile: old staple industries may not fully recover, they may be reshaped with core processes relocated to cheaper countries and employers may begin to hire workers with different skill sets.

The 1980s recession is significant in that it marked a major shift in the industrial shape of the United Kingdom: many manufacturing jobs were permanently lost, and some of the new opportunities created in the service sector resulted in a demand for a new type of employee capable of performing 'emotional work' (Hochschild 1983), in which they were required to become skilled in the use of expressions, such as smiling and eye contact, in their everyday dealings with clients or customers. In this new world, traditional masculinities are sometimes seen as redundant, and even as representing an impediment to employment in the growing sectors of the economy (McDowell 2003). In the new economy, there is a much reduced demand for unskilled industrial workers whose jobs have been either replaced by machines or exported to countries with lower wage costs.

We are currently experiencing the aftermath of another recession, the Great Recession, and we can begin to see the contours of the emerging post-recession economy. In the new order, the flexible employment practices that became more widespread during the recession are retained: workers experience ongoing insecurities, are forced to juggle multiple part-time jobs and are constantly faced with uncertainty about their ability to manage financial commitments. Despite an increasingly qualified workforce, predictions about the growth of jobs point towards the less skilled sectors of the economy, meaning that people are running up large debts for education only to enter a labour market where educated workers are increasingly employed in unskilled jobs. The new labour market is a stratified labour market in which the few enjoy a privileged security while the majority exist under conditions of insecurity. In the new economy, 'precarity is a fundamental condition' (Ball 2013: 134), and the majority become outsiders as part of a *political strategy* to provide differential benefits to the favoured and less favoured (Emmenegger *et al.* 2012: our emphasis).

These changes, which affect people of all ages, have their most profound influence on the lives of young people. Young people tend to bear the brunt of a recession; they are far more likely than older workers to become unemployed and, as new entrants to the labour market, are first to experience the new conditions of the post-recession economy.

In the chapters that follow, we explore the changing experiences of young people from the 1970s to the present day, involving in-depth discussion and analysis of the 1980s recession and the more recent Great Recession. Our discussion is informed by the work of Elias and others outlined here, set within the evolving policy landscapes that frame the lives of young people.

# Chapter 2

# From the 'golden age' to neo-liberalism

Last month the Ministry of Labour told us that 38,000 boys and girls, who left school in July, had not found work. This figure, as we all know, excluded many who, unable to find work, had returned to schools unfitted and ill-equipped to take them back. It excludes, too, the many who found temporary employment in blind-alley jobs. That this country should not be able to find employment for boys and girls leaving school and going out into the world for the first time is an intolerable reflection on our so-called civilisation.

(Harold Wilson's speech to the 1963 Labour Party conference)

## Introduction

Much attention has been given to understanding the consequences of the casualisation of labour in the periods prior to and following the Great Recession (e.g. Standing 2011). While many commentators acknowledge that the roots of the changes were established prior to 2008, few appreciate that, in the United Kingdom and some other European countries, a significant turning point was reached as early as the mid-1970s, with some of the most momentous changes occurring in the early 1980s. To fully understand the contemporary employment contexts experienced by young people, in this chapter we first outline and consider the broader patterns of change and transformation in relation to youth labour markets by considering the employment situations faced by young people in the 1960s and 1970s (a time of relative prosperity with some strain emerging towards the end of the period), before moving on to consider significant changes triggered by the 1980s recession.

Rather than viewing changing labour conditions as an inevitable consequence of economic transformations, we argue that the British state committed a series of civilising offences against young people from the late 1970s, subsequently reinforcing and refining these offences in an ongoing attempt to make young people accept a new set of obligations. Similar actions were carried out in a number of other countries at around the same time as governments began to roll out a neo-liberal political agenda. Acting on behalf of employers, the state introduced a wide range of measures to force workers, especially young workers, to conform to a new set of conditions under which worker rights and welfare benefits were progressively removed to help mobilise the neo-liberal project and normalise emergent fragmented and precarious forms of employment.

To help contextualise and understand the contemporary youth labour market and its direction of travel, it is necessary to draw on an extensive historical canvas in which the post-war labour market is regarded as part of a deep-rooted historical process. Here, we suggest that Norbert Elias's work on the civilising process (2000) and Robert Castel's (2003) work on changes in the organisation of labour and social welfare from medieval to industrial society help us to locate our analysis historically and frame it sociologically. Castel's rich illustration of what he refers to as the 'jeopardization of labor' (2003: 380) traces the demise of the indeterminate contract in France to 1975 and argues that, even before the Great Recession, over two-thirds of new contracts could be classified as 'atypical' (fixed term, part-time or offered under government-sponsored activation programmes): a trend that he recognises as having the greatest impact on women and young people.

To understand the changes that we focus on in the United Kingdom, we have to maintain an awareness that the labour process involves an ongoing subjugation of labour under which the degradation of work constantly evolves in ways that involve new and more exploitative forms (Braverman 1974). Here, the civilising process described by Elias involves changes in the nature of obligations between privileged and subordinate social actors that are held in place by the symbolic violence (Bourdieu 2002) that underpins civilising offences.

## Enforcing conformity in labour relations

Although there is not the space in this volume to provide a deep historical analysis of the period before the 1960s, we would not dissent from Castel's (2003) position regarding changes in the organisation of labour from medieval to industrial society and the relationship between changes in the relationship between welfare and work. Castel describes how in medieval Europe vulnerable citizens, who were often referred to as vagabonds, were brutally treated. In the sixteenth century, in parts of Europe, vagabonds could be subject to immediate execution and in the eighteenth century could be forced to man the galleys in perpetuity (Castel 2003). Then, as now, a distinction was often made between the deserving and undeserving poor, what Castel refers to as the 'shameful poor' and 'able bodied beggars', and favourable treatment reserved for those with strong local connections.

The Black Death (1348–50), which wiped out more than a third of the population of England, caused a labour shortage leading to strong demands for workers. Fearful that this new balance in the supply of and demand for labour may lead to wage rises, the Ordinance of Labour (1349) was passed to limit wages to their pre-plague levels. A series of statutes followed on working conditions and wages, including new attempts to regulate labour in ways that strengthened contractual obligations, such as acts restricting the freedom of workers to join together in an attempt to improve conditions. Following the Black Death, hiring fairs for agricultural workers emerged in many villages, where people would gather in one week at the end of November to seek work for the coming year. Employers had to commit to provide employment for the full year and were, therefore, unable to dispense with the labour they hired in periods of the year when there were relatively few tasks to be carried out on the farm. However, the Master and Servant Act (1823) imposed penalties of up to 3 months' hard labour on any employee who left service before the expiration of the contract. According to Craig (2007), 10,000 people a year were prosecuted under this act. The Master and Servant Act was not repealed until 1867 so, in effect, criminal law underpinned labour relations until that time.

> For most of the past 500 years, employment relations in Britain was governed by the traditional master and servant relationship. Breaches of these contracts were punishable by imprisonment, whipping, fines, forfeiture or compelled labour.
>
> (Craig 2007: 2)

The industrial revolution brought with it new strategies to enforce work discipline, creating obligations for employees to work long, regular hours in return for subsistence wages. Welfare was seen as a key strategy, and employers and politicians were of the view that over-generous provision would make employees reluctant to submit to the harsh working conditions that were common in the manufacturing industry. Indeed, such sentiments were not confined to capitalists and right-wing politicians but were subscribed to by 'liberal' reformers like Beveridge and the Webbs. The Webbs, for example, went as far as to argue that 'an institution where individuals must be criminally regulated and maintained under constraint ... [is] absolutely essential to any effective program of treating unemployment' (Webb and Webb 1911, quoted in Castel 2003).

The Beveridge Report that underpinned the Labour Party's approach to developing a welfare state in the post-Second World War era was also concerned to ensure that workers conformed to employers' demands, and the insurance-based system he proposed was to provide a fairly comprehensive safety net to those who acted in accordance with his model of the 'good worker, regular in his labor and disciplined in his morals' (Castel 2003: 308).

For centuries, welfare and labour discipline have been two sides of the same coin, and the evolution of the forms of obligation between employer and employee and between state and citizen represents a core component of the civilising process proposed by Elias. However, for Elias, civilising processes are seen as 'long-term, intergenerational, unplanned and unintended processes, involving changes in the balance of the typical social habitus' (Mennell 2015: n.p.), whereas the history of labour relations is littered with what Elias refers to as civilising offences. As discussed in the previous chapter, civilising offences are planned processes and may take the form of an offence against those who rely on welfare (Clement 2015) or an offence against younger citizens to force them to conform to a form of labour discipline favoured by the state.

Conformity is also underpinned by a hegemonic discourse that shames groups of workers who are regarded as problematic. A process of shaming has underpinned approaches to welfare since the middle ages and continues to this day, as governments and the popular media link unemployment to what they claim to be deficits in attitudes, ethics or skills. Examples include a speech by Norman Tebbit, a minister in Margaret Thatcher's government, claiming that a reluctance on the part of the unemployed to 'get on their bikes' in search of work outside their locality was evidence of a culture of welfare reliance. Similar claims were made by Chris Grayling in the Cameron administration, who argued that in some families several generations had never worked, while contemporary discourses accuse immigrant populations of coming to the United Kingdom to claim benefits rather than work.

There are also discourses that centre on the idea of employability, whereby individuals are seen as lacking in various attributes demanded by employers. The focus here tends to be on a deficit of skills, including soft skills, which make someone unemployable. Clearly some people lack the skills to perform certain tasks or display traits that employers feel will not be conducive to maintaining the customer-focused image they wish to project. At the same time, we must recognise that demands for skills and behavioural standards are not fixed, but are differently defined according to predominant modes of production and levels of employment. In agrarian society, employability was defined in terms of physical ability; in industrial society, it was about the ability to conform to the demands of regular monotonous work and long-hours cultures; in contemporary society, it may be about an ability to manage complex and fragmented working lives and cope with an all-pervasive sense of insecurity. Moreover, it is important to appreciate that the same person may be regarded as highly employable in a buoyant labour market but seen as unemployable at times or in places where jobs are more scarce.

## The 1960s: Young people and work in the 'golden age'?

The 1960s is often considered to be a 'golden age' (Vickerstaff 2003), in which jobs were plentiful and unemployment short-lived. According to Roberts and colleagues, in many parts of Britain 'virtually all school-leavers stepped directly into jobs' (1986: n.p.): a situation that he illustrates using his personal experiences in the opening chapter. With low levels of geographical mobility among young people, the sorts of jobs available to them varied considerably from one locality to the next, and, as Goodwin and O'Connor (2005) showed in their reanalysis of data from the period, not all local labour markets were characterised by their prosperity: indeed, they argue that the use of the term 'golden age' to refer to the 1960s is misleading. Prior to the 1980s recession, many openings involved manual work, with conditions and prospects varying according to the industrial make-up of an area and opportunities for training.

In the 1971 census, overall, more than six in ten males and four in ten females worked in manual occupations, and the professional sector offered relatively few opportunities, especially for females. Among 15- to 19-year-olds, seven in ten males and one-third of females worked in manual occupations (Table 2.1). The 1960s and 1970s was an era where minimum-aged school leaving was the norm, especially among those whose families worked in manual occupations, and the very small numbers who went to university were all but guaranteed careers in the professional and managerial sectors (Ashton and Field 1976).

In the 1970s, around one in four young people entered apprenticeships, while one around one in five entered clerical occupations (Banks and Ullah 1988) that typically involved some firm- or sector-specific training and offered the possibility of a degree of career advancement (Ashton and Field 1976). However, during the 1970s, and linked to the decline of manufacturing industries, the availability of apprenticeships declined, removing many of the traditional opportunities open for young people from working-class families to develop marketable skills and enhance their future job security.

Table 2.1 Employment of the economically active population, 1971

|  | All-age | | 15–19 | |
| --- | --- | --- | --- | --- |
|  | Males | Females | Males | Females |
| Management and professional | 5 | 1 | 1 | 0 |
| Intermediate | 17 | 16 | 5 | 7 |
| Skilled non-manual | 11 | 37 | 13 | 53 |
| Skilled manual | 38 | 10 | 44 | 13 |
| Semi-skilled | 17 | 25 | 16 | 20 |
| Unskilled | 8 | 7 | 10 | 1 |
| Unclassified | 3 | 4 | 10 | 6 |

Source: UK Population Census, 1971, quoted in Roberts et al. 1986.

Writing in the early 1970s and drawing on data collected in the 1960s, Ashton and Field (1976) focused on the ways in which young people adjusted to the world of work. They argued that social background had a major impact on the meanings that people attached to work and, with expectations conditioned by social class and educational experiences, few young people experienced severe problems of adjustment. They suggested that

> most young people do *not* experience the transition from school to work as a period of particular stress or as involving them in traumatic problems of adjustment to their new position in the adult community. Rather, it appears that the previous experience of the young people in their home, school and peer group prepares them well to fit in or adjust to the demands imposed upon them on starting work.
>
> (Ashton and Field 1976: 12, original italics)

For Ashton and Field (1976), transitions from school to work were highly stratified, with most young people following clearly defined tracks through education into different sectors of the labour market: tracks which were strongly conditioned by their social class background. Drawing on economic and cultural resources, young people from middle-class families learnt how to exercise initiative and were taught to defer immediate rewards in order to focus on long-term gains.

The possession of middle-class cultural capital, Bourdieu (1977) asserted, helped ensure that those from advantaged social backgrounds received a privileged education either in the state sector or in the private sector. In turn, the qualifications gained from this privileged educational route helped ensure that the majority were placed in either managerial and professional or white-collar professions, either directly or following an additional period of study in further or higher education. In contrast, young people from the middle and lower working classes tended to be channelled through the lower streams of the school into semi- and unskilled manual jobs at the minimum leaving age of 15 or 16, while those from upper working-class families were often placed in the upper streams of the school, where they gained the qualifications that would help them secure apprenticeships for skilled craft work or else they found routine white-collar positions (Figure 2.1).

Under these conditions, there were clear linkages between the family, school and labour market, with employment prospects being highly predictable. Indeed, sociologists like Paul Willis (1977) outlined a process through which young men effectively embraced subordinate positions within the labour market. For Willis, manual occupations were an opportunity for young men from working-class families to assert their masculinity, while white-collar jobs were rejected due to a perceived requirement for obedience and conformity. For Ashton and Field (1976), the labour

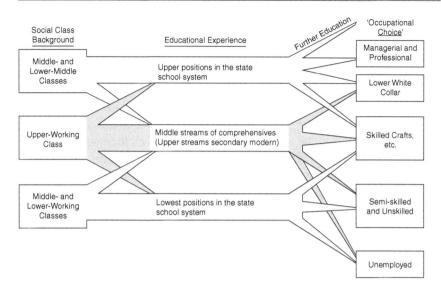

*Figure 2.1* Social class background, school experience and 'occupational choice'
Source: Ashton and Field 1976.

market was clearly segmented, with little movement between sectors; managerial and professional, lower white-collar and skilled manual employment required fairly specific educational credentials and job-specific training. For those without qualifications or job-related (usually apprentice) training, most opportunities were in semi- and unskilled forms of employment, and the chances of mobility to other, more secure and better paid segments were relatively poor. In the early 1970s, around a third of young people entered jobs that offered little or no training, with many of these jobs being low-paid and insecure (Banks and Ullah 1988).

With transitions from school to work in the so-called golden age often regarded by contemporary commentators as smooth and predictable, and marked by relatively full employment, the era is sometimes used as a benchmark to highlight the complexity that characterised experiences from the late 1970s onwards. However, this has to be qualified by the acknowledgement that mobility was severely restricted, while opportunities for lower working-class youth were heavily concentrated in low-skill, low-paid work. Moreover, both Goodwin and O'Connor (2005) and Vickerstaff (2003) have argued that employment in this era was often more complex than previously thought, with job changing frequent and periods of unemployment not uncommon. Goodwin and O'Connor, for example, showed that some of the young workers in the Leicester area were changing jobs as frequently as monthly. Despite relatively full employment, for some, the fear of unemployment was an issue that shaped their actions. As Goodwin and O'Connor argue, 'Past transitional experiences were not uniformly simple, linear or as single step as previously suggested and many transitions were characterised by individual level complexities similar to those of contemporary youth' (2005: 218).

While Goodwin and O'Connor provide rich examples of young people's movements between semi- and unskilled jobs, around a third of male school leavers secured apprenticeships which were associated with lower levels of job changing. Apprenticeships tended to involve a 5-year commitment which, for many, was regarded as an awfully long period in which they were relatively poorly paid (Vickerstaff 2003). Young apprentices were often treated harshly and regularly encountered behaviour from older workers that today would be regarded as unacceptable. The idea that young people moved smoothly and untraumatically from the school into the workplace runs counter to the evidence that emerged from contemporary sources. To quote from one of the apprentices cited by Vickerstaff,

> It was the worst six years of my life. Every morning I used to dread getting up and going into this place … It was name-calling. Taking the Mickey – 'Long streak of piss' and all this sort of thing because I was only about ten and a half stone and already six foot three. I became a nervous wreck in a way. And I never told my Mum and Dad about it because you didn't do. I used to come out in the lunch break to cycle home and the bike would be turned upside down, the tyres let down, two or three times a week.
>
> (2003: 278)

Moreover, although employment was relatively full, this did not mean that young people were able to exercise choice. Young workers were constrained by local opportunity structures, and demand for apprenticeships was always higher than supply. Young people who entered the labour market at 15 or 16 were often treated as children, both by their families and by fellow workers – male apprentices were commonly referred to as 'the boy' – and parents frequently made career decisions on behalf of their offspring (Vickerstaff 2003; Goodwin and O'Connor 2005).

While young people frequently entered the type of employment that they had said that they had wanted while at school (Maizels 1970), their aspirations were clearly shaped by local opportunity structures and their position in the stratified world of the school (Roberts 1975). Indeed, West and Newton (1983) were highly critical of schools' use of a developmental approach to careers guidance which encouraged greater occupational ambition. Such an approach, they argued, subsequently led to a downward adjustment and disappointment. West and Newton argued that a 'developmental approach merely aggravates and exacerbates the difficulties faced by adolescents in adjusting to the opportunity structures which exists in the world of work. [It] ignores the reality of high levels of unemployment, of the stress and drudgery of work' (1983: 183).

Despite the predictability of occupational attainment, starting work was a time of surprises; good and bad. Studies report initial surprise at the some of the freedoms of the workplace (such as being able to smoke and walk about to talk to others) but also surprise at the level of boredom to be tolerated, the physical strain of some of the work and the long working hours (Carter 1962; West and Newton 1983). Young people often had very little idea of what to expect on their first day at work and were provided with scant formal inductions. In West and Newton's (1983) study, around 45 per cent of respondents said that their introduction to the work and the firm was either non-existent or lasted less than 30 minutes. Maizels (1970) found that half of the new workers were shown what to do by a fellow worker – a common form of training sometimes described as 'sitting next to Nellie'.

While relative wages of young people in the 1960s have been regarded as healthy and linked to the emergence of the teenage consumer (Abrams 1959), by the late 1970s average wages for school leavers were quite low. In West and Newton's (1983) study, for example, 9 months after leaving school nearly six in ten 17-year-olds were paid between £21 and £30 per week: adjusted for inflation, a point midway through this range equates to £136, which is about what a 17-year-old on the minimum age would be paid in 2014. Moreover, female wages were significantly lower than male wages (one in four females earned less than £20 per week, compared to one in ten males, and while 16 per cent of males earned more than £39 a week, no females in their study earned this amount) (West and Newton 1983).

Another important point to make, especially when reflecting on debates concerning the emergence of a so-called precariat (Standing 2011) in the late modern era, is that piecework, where employees' wages were directly determined by personal productivity, was extremely common in some sectors of the economy, such as the textile industry. In West and Newton's (1983) study, more than three in ten females were paid on a piecework formula. A long-hours culture was also common, with many young people working regular overtime to secure reasonable wages levels.

## From the oil crisis to economic recession

Although writing in the early to mid-1970s, Ashton and Field were effectively describing a context that characterised the 1960s (they were drawing on data from the 1950s and early 1960s) which was about to be severely disrupted. The 1973 oil crisis, triggered by the Organisation of Petroleum Exporting Countries (OPEC) in an attempt to use their control over oil prices to enhance the economic development of their countries, led to a fourfold increase in oil prices, triggering a wage-price inflationary spiral in the West that resulted in manufacturing uncertainty and reduced production which, in turn, had a detrimental impact on levels of employment.

From the 1970s onwards, the manufacturing base of the UK economy was eroded with a reduction in output and jobs. This trend was particularly severe from the late 1970s and in the recession of the early 1980s. From 1978 to 1983, manufacturing output declined by 30 per cent (ONS 2006), while between 1980 and 1983 a third of the manual jobs in engineering were lost (Maguire 1991). While the same period saw an increase in jobs in the service industries, the rise was of a lower magnitude, with many of the posts being created being part-time and filled by women (Maguire 1991). These trends led to an increase in the proportion of females in employment and the narrowing of the gap in participation between men and women.

Economic uncertainty, new sources of competition and industrial restructuring led to a rise in all-age unemployment from the early to the late 1970s. Youth unemployment also began to rise in the 1970s stimulated by the demographic bulge caused by the coming of age of the baby boomers (Berger 1989) but, as among older people, also affected by the impact of the oil crisis on labour demand and by the acceleration of a shift from manufacturing to service-based employment and the associated demand for better educated and customer-friendly workers. All-age unemployment, which stood at 2.6 per cent in 1970, had risen to 6.9 per cent by 1977 (Jackson 1985), while youth unemployment rose from 2.9 per cent in 1970 to 15.3 per cent by 1980 (Jackson 1985) (Figure 2.2). Long-term unemployment among young people more than doubled between 1979 and 1982, accounting for just over one in five of those registered unemployed (Junankar 1987).

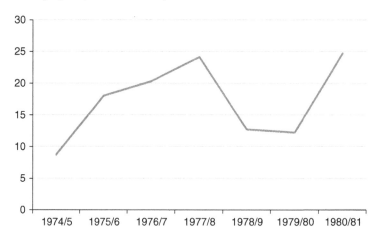

*Figure 2.2* School leaver unemployment, England and Wales, 1974/5 to 1980/1

Source: Derived from figures in Jackson 1985.

A rise in unemployment is always a serious issue for young people as they are more likely than older people to be affected and likely to experience a longer duration. Indeed, for a variety of reasons, youth unemployment is usually far higher than among older age groups (typically three times higher) (Makeham 1980). Makeham has argued that young people experience higher levels of unemployment because

- They are more likely to be seeking work than older people as they display higher levels of job changing and may be trying to secure a first job after leaving education.
- They may be excluded from a range of occupations, some of which have age restrictions.
- When employers shed labour, young people may be affected by 'last-in, first-out' policies.

Moreover, young people with few qualifications are far more likely than their qualified peers to experience unemployment and tend to be unemployed for much longer periods of time.

The industrial changes that were occurring throughout the 1970s and which were accelerated in the 1980s recession had been predicted in a speech made by Harold Wilson to the Labour Party conference in 1963. In what was commonly referred to as the 'white heat of technology' speech, Wilson drew attention to the growth in youth unemployment and warned of the need to develop 'a totally new attitude to the problem of apprenticeship, of training and re-training for skill' (1963: 7), and of the need to provide enhanced and more socially just education for young people so as to prepare a 'Britain that is going to be forged in the white heat of this revolution' (1963: 7).

The Wilson government placed a high priority on education: committing a higher proportion of GDP to education, his government drove through an ambitious programme of university expansion, established 29 polytechnics and the Open University and began to replace grammar and secondary modern schools with comprehensive schools in an attempt to reduce the early stratification of educational experiences which was regarded as reproducing working-class disadvantage (Jackson and Marsden 1962; Douglas 1967). Despite these moves, in the early 1980s, the United Kingdom was still a country where minimum-age school leaving was extremely common and in which higher education remained a minority experience. In Scotland in 1981, for example, 57 per cent of males and 52 per cent of females left school at the minimum age, and a minority obtained the five plus O grades that are considered to be an indicator of a satisfactory secondary experience (Furlong 1992). Among those born in the United Kingdom in 1958, upon reaching the age of 23, in 1981, just 10 per cent had obtained university degrees (Fogelman 1985).

Recognising that the United Kingdom was lagging behind other countries, such as the United States, in school retention, the school-leaving age was raised to 16 in England and Wales in 1972. However, the increase in educational participation, which extended to upper secondary and tertiary education, was already on the rise and was largely driven by external factors rather than policy. Changes in opportunities, which included a growing shortage of employers recruiting young people for both low-skill jobs and apprenticeships, together with demands for more advanced qualifications, helped encourage higher levels of educational participation. The so-called discouraged worker effect can be linked to rising levels of unemployment and to the introduction of new types of government-sponsored work experience and training schemes (Raffe and Williams 1989).

## Youth schemes: responding to growing youth unemployment

Coming after a long period of relatively full employment, the rising level of youth unemployment from the early 1970s onwards was very visible, fuelling calls for political action. Indeed, moral panics linked to prevalent youth cultures led to a heightened concern about 'idle hands'. In a sense, government intervention in this period was linked to fears about increasing levels of hooliganism and delinquency triggered by unemployment (Sinfield 1981). As Osgerby noted, the mid-1970s were marked by 'an air of crisis and social polarization' (1998: 104).

Despite Harold Wilson's earlier acknowledgement that adverse economic conditions were not fully captured by formal unemployment rates but extended to temporary employment in 'blind-alley jobs' and reluctant returns to education, the focus of policy makers and the media was on visible unemployment rather than on young people in insecure jobs or out of sight and off the political radar in full-time education.

With a clear focus on those formally unemployed, in 1975 the Job Creation Programme was established to maintain and enhance young people's employability through the creation of short-term jobs of social value. This scheme, which was the first in a series of schemes developed to cater for young people without work, was underpinned by the view that the rise in youth unemployment was temporary and that measures needed to be introduced to occupy school leavers and provide them with some experience until an economic upturn made the measures redundant.

This interpretation was challenged by the publication of the Holland Report in 1977 which promoted the view that youth unemployment was structural and linked to changing patterns of demand. While Holland was clear that youth unemployment was primarily caused by a deficit in demand, the report also carried a message suggesting that new skill sets were needed which unemployed young people often lacked. In response to the Holland Report, the government introduced a new programme, the Youth Opportunities Programme (YOP), which was designed to 'enable the individual to do more things, achieve a higher level of skills, knowledge and performance, and adapt more readily to changing circumstances or job requirements' (Holland 1977: 33).

YOP was a 6-month programme of work experience targeted at 16- and 17-year-olds who had been unemployed for a minimum of 6 months. Participants were paid an allowance which was set marginally above the unemployment rate. While Holland had hoped to steer the government towards the introduction of enhanced training provision for a post-industrial age, in practice the programme provided little in the way of 'hard' job-related skills but focused on the enhancement of 'soft skills', particularly those related to workplace discipline and conformity, thus reinforcing the view that youth unemployment was linked to poor work-related attitudes and values.

Representing an early civilising offensive against young people, YOP marked a real sea-change in transitions from school to work, as YOP soon became a majority experience. In Britain at the time, around 700,000 young people moved from school to the labour market each year; of these, by its fourth year of operation, around 550,000 entered the programme (Raffe 1981).

For Holland, though, unemployment was not a personal failing but could be linked to the poor state of the national economy. Indeed,

> Success or failure in getting the job is often a matter of luck and frequently determined by factors well beyond the control or achievement of the individual such as the state of the national economy, the local industrial structure or the kind of preparation for work available at school. Unemployed young people are not failures: they are those whom others have so far failed.
>
> (Holland 1977: 33)

However, Raffe (1981) has argued that implicit in the Holland Report was an acceptance of the basic tenets of human capital theory:

> that individual productivity and labour market success are determined by personal qualities which can be created by investment in education or similar provision. YOPs approach is therefore based at least partly on an individualist explanation of unemployment which attributes it to the individual deficiencies of the unemployed'.
>
> (1981: 217)

The ways in which the debate on youth unemployment, its causes and its remedies is framed have clear consequences for the actions expected of young people. If unemployment is seen as linked to personal shortcomings, then there may be a legitimate expectation that they take advantage of any opportunities provided to address these deficits. However, if unemployment is regarded as structural, as a matter of luck, then individuals may rightly feel an entitlement to unconditional compensation.

The period of relatively full employment that existed prior to the mid-1970s, in which periods of unemployment tended to be short-lived, was marked by a fairly sympathetic benefit culture in which assumptions about entitlements prevailed. For those who had worked long enough in the previous financial year, unemployment benefits were linked to National Insurance contributions, with supplementary benefits providing additional support to meet specific needs (such as dependents). There was also an earnings-related supplement (introduced in 1966) which provided additional sums to claimants based on the level of their past earnings. With a sense of entitlement to levels of compensation that would provide those without work with a reasonable standard of living, in the 1960s and 1970s claimants unions were formed in many parts of the country, often affiliated to the Federation of Claimants Unions, which held an annual conference. The aim was to support 'claimants helping each other to claim what we can from the welfare state' and demanding 'a basic income for all' (Radical History Network 2009: n.p.). Although involvement was not widespread, their existence highlights a broader culture under which people expected that the state would meet their basic needs if they were unable to find work.

Although young people were often ineligible for anything other than basic-level benefits, prior to the introduction of YOP unemployed 16-year-old school leavers were eligible to claim benefits more or less as soon as they left school. Relatively few did so, because in many parts of the country jobs were relatively plentiful. In Carter's (1962) study, which was carried out between 1959 and 1960, and in a later study by West and Newton (1983) using data collected from 1976 to 1979, around half of all school leavers found jobs before they left school: and around four in ten said that they had a choice of jobs. Moreover, the availability of benefits and the existence of a relatively lax regime did not encourage young people to sign on rather than accepting a job considered to be second best or of poor quality. In West and Newton's study, around 30 per cent of school leavers accepted a job for negative reasons, such as a perception that there was nothing else available or because they were frightened of not being able to get a job.

The introduction of YOP marked the beginning of a new era for youth benefits: although there was no evidence of abuse of the system or of large numbers of young people opting to remain on benefits in preference to entering even poorly paid jobs, from here on young people were expected to demonstrate their willingness to work by taking part in programmes without marked financial gain, without being provided with quality training and without evidence that participation would improve their future prospects. Understandably, this led to widespread resentment among young people who often described YOP as 'slave labour' (Stafford 1981). Young people often begrudged working for an employer who made no contribution towards their allowance, made no commitment to offer them paid work in the future and provided them with very little in the way of credible training or the development of marketable skills.

Beginning with YOP, but intensifying under later schemes, punitive regimes were implemented whereby refusal of a placement, even where travel was difficult or the placement showed no respect for their interests or qualifications, led to sanctions in the form of benefit withdrawal. A relatively sympathetic system of support for young people without jobs had been transformed into one underpinned by suspicion and sanctions – a move we refer to as the 'punitive turn', representing the first of a series of civilising offensives in the post-war era committed against young people to force them to accept a new set of obligations.

Hence, the deterioration in conditions for young people observed as recession that set in during the early 1980s led to an acceleration of trends already visible by the end of the 1970s. Unemployment was already an issue for young people making the transition from school to work, and many were forced to spend time on government training programmes before moving into 'proper jobs'. Benefit regimes had already become more punitive, and the state had begun to take a more directive role in shaping opportunities and setting expectations. While young people themselves had begun to regard education as a refuge in a difficult labour market, the government had also learnt that pushing young people into education and training schemes was a very effective way of reducing politically sensitive youth unemployment rates.

## The shift to the political right

Against a backdrop of economic and industrial turmoil in the 1970s, underpinned by the 1973 oil crisis, the emerging impact of economic globalisation and the significant decline in the United Kingdom's traditional industries, national politics took a drastic shift to the political right. It is important to understand this shift to the right, given the consequences it would have for work and employment – consequences that are still experienced today – and the fact that industrial and employment policies from 1979 would provide the basis for future precarious forms of employment. As previously discussed, traditional forms of work and employment were clearly changing from the early the 1970s; however, this transformation was to accelerate dramatically in the 1980s with the election of Margaret Thatcher's Conservative government in 1979. The ongoing industrial disputes towards the end of the 1970s, the perceived monopoly of the trade unions, the drastic impact of government spending cuts, imposed and insisted upon by the International

Monetary Fund in 1976, and increasing inflation lead to a weary British public seeking political change. As the Conservative Party (1979) suggested,

> This Election is about the future of Britain – a great country which seems to have lost its way. What has happened to our country, to the values we used to share, to the success and prosperity we once took for granted? During the industrial strife of last winter, confidence, self-respect, common sense, and even our sense of common humanity were shaken. At times this society seemed on the brink of disintegration … by enlarging the role of the State and diminishing the role of the individual, [The Labour Party] have crippled the enterprise and effort on which a prosperous country with improving social services depends … by heaping privilege without responsibility on the trade unions, Labour have given a minority of extremists the power to abuse individual liberties and to thwart Britain's chances of success.
>
> (Conservative Party Manifesto 1979)

Thatcher's analysis of the period from the mid-1960s, a period in which the Labour Party had held power for all but 4 years, was that the balance of power had shifted in favour of the 'state' at the expense of individual freedoms, that the state was too involved in the lives of 'ordinary people' who, instead, should be encouraged to become part of a 'property owning democracy'. It held that the trade unions had become too powerful and required reform, that social welfare was too expensive and that government policy should shift away from the state underwriting the welfare state and promising full employment while maintaining control of inflation and spending. Further, it asserted that deregulation, de-nationalisation and industry based on the pursuit of profit were essential for future prosperity rather than the state and taxpayer trying to preserve existing jobs through subsidies. The electorate returned the Conservative Party to power with 43.9 per cent of the popular vote, and a majority of 70 members of Parliament, ensuring that their radical, right-wing, monetarist policy reorientation would mean that the next decade came to be characterised by unprecedented social and economic transformation that would impact on the lives of all those living in the United Kingdom. Such trends were repeated elsewhere, such as in the United States, where Reagan's neo-conservatives adopted fully the neo-liberal mantra that combined the further 'rolling back of the state' and a greater emphasis on market forces and consumerism.

At the forefront of these change were young people, who were seriously affected as the old certainties of *relatively* straightforward school-to-work transitions disappeared and the number of apprenticeships were dramatically reduced as manufacturing industry was decimated. Young people were at the vanguard of economic and social change due to a ready acceptance by the state that unemployment, and particularly youth unemployment, was a necessary 'corrective' to the supply and demand problems experienced in the UK labour market throughout the 1970s (a corrective that was regarded as likely to be a short-term one). During the 1980s, young people were to be subject to the vagaries of *Special Employment Measures* and the *Youth Training Scheme* (YTS) that embodied 'the essence of Thatcherism ... that aimed to give school leavers opportunities to price themselves back into jobs' (Lee *et al.* 1990: 3), essentially by lowering wages and offering remedial interventions to change youth attitudes to work, forcing them to take personal responsibility for their unemployed status. Where jobs were available, they were increasingly part-time, temporary, short-term, low skilled and low-paid, laying the foundations for the following decades. In short, the traditional work undertaken by young people and the seemingly 'usual jobs' they entered, plus the routes via which they transitioned to the labour market, were being replaced by something increasingly precarious.

## The consolidation of youth training schemes

Between 1951 and 1981 unemployment rates for young people under eighteen years increased from 1 per cent to about 25 per cent. Without the Youth Training Scheme and Special Employment Measures, the current youth unemployment rate might well be nearer to 50 per cent.

(Hart 1988: 1)

A key response to the significant growth in youth unemployment by the Conservative government, elected in 1979, was the introduction of a variety of YTS as an extension and refinement of the YOP introduced by the previous political administration (see Finn 1987; Ashton *et al.* 1990: Lee *et al.* 1990) and which ran between 1978 and 1983. As discussed earlier, YOP was introduced in order to provide employment preparation through work preparation courses, training courses and employer-based work experiences spread over a 12-month period (Finn 1987: 111). In return, the young person received between £18 and £19.50 per week. As Ryan (1989: 175) suggests, by 1980 a place was guaranteed on the scheme for all jobless 16-year-old school leavers, and Ryan highlights that by 1980/81, 98 per cent of all 16-year-olds in the labour force were on YTS (which equates to 39 per cent of the total population of 16-year-olds). Yet, as Conservative minister Alan Clark (1993) recognised in 1983, the programme was seen as little more than 'tacky schemes' designed to massage the youth unemployment figures. Moreover, Morgan (1981) and others report that bodies such as the Trades Union Congress had begun to question the value of YOP in terms of the quality of the training being delivered and as a mechanism for lowering wages, despite their initial support for the scheme. As Mizen (1990) elaborates,

> It was being increasingly claimed that YOP was no more than a cosmetic measure, designed mainly to keep young people off the unemployment statistics, raising their aspirations only to return them to the dole .... The quality of work experience and training came under sharp scrutiny as over 3,000 accidents were recorded during YOP's lifetime, including five fatalities and 23 amputations.
>
> (Mizen 1990: 18)

Widespread dissatisfaction with the YOP led to a re-working and re-branding of the scheme as the YTS in 1983 following the *Youth Task Group Report* of the Manpower Services Commission (MSC) in 1982. The *Youth Task Group Report* signalled a break with the past (Lee *et al*. 1990), and YTS became positioned as a 'new deal' for both the young unemployed and employers, and as an employer/market-led training programme increasingly free from the interference of trades unions. It also represented something of a staged transition from school to work (see Raffe 1990), replacing the relatively single-step transitions of the 1950s and 1960s.

Despite government claims that YTS represented a real break with earlier approaches, like previous schemes YTS was a substitute for 'real jobs' and, like YOP, was perceived to offer little benefit to participants beyond moving them from the unemployment register (in return for minimal financial gain). Likewise, it was dogged with the perception of being about cheap labour and poor-quality training, with the Trades Union Congress labelling YTS as a 'youth training swindle'. These limitations were also well understood by the young people themselves, and one does not have to search very far within research from that time to find the negative impact that YTS was having on young people.

Contemporary research also shows that, for many, participation often provided little in the way of new opportunities. As Ashton and colleagues (1990) showed, the introduction of free labour through youth training had little impact on the range of jobs available to 16-year-olds: those that were marginalised before the training remained marginalised afterwards. Nor did the scheme help address social divisions, and many have suggested that YTS actually served to reinforce processes of marginalisation. According to Cockburn (1987), YTS did little more than underpin existing patterns of sex-based occupational segregation, with young women being heavily concentrated in YTS occupational areas associated with caring, health, personal services and sales. Likewise, the social divisions built up around race and ethnicity with regard to employment were exacerbated by the scheme, whereby those from ethnic minorities were often placed on poor quality programmes.

> Young blacks in inner London are being forced into a Youth Training Scheme 'ghetto' while young whites from the suburbs get most of the jobs in the City and West End, according to the Inner London Education Authority. The figures show a much higher take-up of YTS places by young Afro-Caribbeans, than other ethnic groups.
>
> (The *Guardian*, 26 January 1987)

In relation to social class, YTS offered little to those young people from working-class families. Underpinning the rhetoric around YTS was a belief by the Conservative government that young working-class youth, in particular, had to lift their horizons beyond the decaying industries and become more entrepreneurial, aspirational, self-reliant and industrious. If they were none of these things then they were characterised as lazy, idle; as scroungers who had nobody but themselves to blame for their unemployed status. Yet, young people themselves frequently resisted attempts to blame them for being unemployed (Lee *et al*. 1987; Mizen 1990), recognising that their unemployment was in part due to the very existence of YTS as a substitute employment scheme. Ashton's analysis went further, arguing that YTS reinforced and replicated class division as 'middle class youth continue in higher education and the YTS becomes a measure utilised by working class youth' (1986: 181), with the skills they obtained simply replicating those they had already acquired through part-time working, through school or via interactions with their parents (Mizen 1990).

The poor training and poor work offered through YTS was no substitute for the quality training previously available relatively widely through apprenticeships. Indeed, McKie (1989) concludes that 'the nature of that training was markedly different in content and outcome when compared with the apprenticeship programmes of earlier decades. Job specific skills and opportunities to undertake widely recognised qualifications are available to few YTS trainees' (McKie 1989: 382). For the majority, YTS did not offer meaningful work, and the scheme did little to address the real problem of the lack of quality jobs for young people in the labour market.

Participation on YTS also had a long-term impact. For example, using a sample of 2,000 low achievers (those with academic qualifications equivalent to the three lowest National Vocational Qualification levels) from the 2000 British Cohort Study longitudinal survey, Dolton and colleagues (2004) found that the wage and employment effects were large and negative for men, with the mean earnings for ex-YTS participants being over 8 per cent lower and employment rates 8.5 per cent lower than a comparable low-achieving cohort of men who did not participate in the YTS scheme. They also suggested that the ex-YTS males had all spent a longer time unemployed than the comparator group. The short-term labour market interventions of either YOP or YTS enhanced precarity rather than resolved it.

## The growth of non-standard employment

By the early 1970s, in many industrialised economies of the West, early school leavers had lost the prospect of transitioning to permanent full-time paid employment, with one or two life-time employers. Although in the 1980s it was still the case that the majority of those in work were engaged as full-time, permanent employees, there was, alongside, a significant increase in the numbers of workers who were employed in a 'non-standard' way. If the standard during the 'golden age' of employment can be defined as full-time and permanent, then 'non-standard' typifies part-time, temporary, flexible zero hours contracts as well as a variety of forms of self-employment. This trend towards non-standard working accelerated in the 1980s, with non-standard forms of work starting to become a substitute for permanent full time work.

In many respects, the growth of non-standard working was a direct consequence of government polices since 1979 and the desire to improve economic performance through deregulation and increased flexibility for employers. This trend had significant implications for young workers who, in a context of rising youth unemployment, were increasingly under pressure to take non-standard forms of employment. Indeed, figures from the Labour Force Survey show that the number of part-time workers aged 16–19 trebled between 1979 and 1985, with more than 400,000 young workers in part-time work by the mid-1980s (Youthaid 1986).

---

There has been a 250 per cent increase since 1979 in the number of teenagers in part-time work. [...] By 1985, one in four teenagers could find only a part-time job. Nearly half the teenagers in part-time work have jobs that are temporary.

(The *Times*, 18 December 1986)

---

Drawing on later figures from the Labour Force Survey (Figure 2.3), Felstead and colleagues (1997) show an increase in non-standard employment among 15- to 24-year-olds between the late 1980s and early 1990s. The numbers in non-standard employment increased by around 10 percentage points, with a particularly pronounced increase in the numbers of females holding multiple jobs, suggesting that many of those in part-time employment wanted more hours.

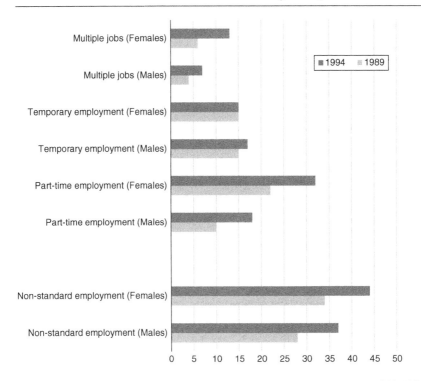

*Figure 2.3* Young people aged 15–24 engaged in non-standard employment: 1989, 1994

Source: Derived from Felstead, A., Krahn, H. and Powell, M. (1997) using data from the Labour Force Survey 1989 and the Quarterly Labour Force Survey Spring 1994.

## Conclusion

Without an appreciation of the changes occurring in the 1970s and 1980s, we could believe that the conditions experienced by young people today can be linked to current economic conditions and a transformation of employment contexts that occurred in the last 10 or 20 years. There is evidence, as we shall discuss in later chapters, of an escalation of trends at around the time of the Great Recession, but in reality the insecurities faced by young people today have deep historical roots. Although the 'jeopardization of labour' (Castel 2003) can be traced back to antiquity and moved through various phases, we can identify a new phase that began in the 1970s, linked to the emerging neo-liberal project championed by Margaret Thatcher. While this involved a laissez-faire approach to the economy underpinned by privatisation, deregulation and a reduction in the tax burden, it also involved an unprecedented level of government intervention in the youth labour market. These interventions were not limited to the provision of training schemes, but also involved the introduction of increasingly punitive welfare systems under which benefits were made conditional on demonstrations of obedience, conformity and 'positive' attitude.

Of course, even without the political drivers, the 1970s and 1980s was a period of substantial restructuring involving the virtual decimation of the manufacturing industry with the loss of traditional jobs for working-class young men, the growth of a feminised service sector which challenged conventional masculinities and demands for emotional labour that placed new pressures on young women and men. The era was also characterised by the introduction of new contractual arrangements, largely in the form of an increased prevalence of part-time contracts in the service sectors, as the routine use of simple technologies, such as electronic cash registers, made employers much more aware of the ebbs and flows in customer demand.

The politics of the period was marked by crisis management. Economic decline and inflation were causes for concern throughout much of the 1960s, with the loss of export markets and problems with balance of payments leading to the devaluation of the pound in 1967 and squeezes on consumer credit. The United Kingdom entered the 1970s with low unemployment rates, but following the 1973 oil crisis the economy was under strain, and industrial relations were fraught. The measures introduced in the mid-1970s to address growing concerns about youth unemployment set the scene for a progression of largely ineffective measures which tended to have a common thread: a tendency to see youth as at fault for their predicament, introducing a series of civilising offensives against young people in the form of increasingly harsh sanctions to deal with those who experienced difficulties moving from the unemployment register to employment and the development of underfunded and unambitious forms of training running in parallel with lucrative opportunities for privatised contractors. The election of Margaret Thatcher in 1979 led to an escalation of these trends and a new set of assaults on the rights of workers that had been won since the early nineteenth century.

The 1970s and 1980s was also an era in which experiential divisions opened up within families, with forms of youth culture making visible contrasting interests and orientations that can be linked to different experiences in education and the labour market. While the parents of those entering the labour market in the 1970s had often grown up in a period of relative affluence and employment stability, young people entering the labour market at the end of the period were having to negotiate a different set of circumstances to those experienced by their parents. Whereas their parents had made transitions within relatively tight parameters, on both objective and subjective levels, for their children who left school from the mid-1970s onwards, the negotiation of pathways, many of which were new, had started to become more confusing and complex. Old road maps had become unhelpful, the signs were more difficult to interpret and parents were less able to offer effective guidance to their offspring (Furlong and Cartmel 1997).

# Chapter 3

# The great transformation and the punitive turn

> The gradual retrenchment of the social welfare state after the mid-1970s is another major political cause of the continued deterioration of the life chances of the urban (sub)proletariat [...]. Contrary to popular neoconservative rhetoric [...], the last quarter of the century was not a period of expansion and generosity for welfare but one of blanket retraction.
>
> (Waquant 2008: 80)

## Introduction

Without a doubt, the experience of leaving school and starting work was transformed during the 1970s and 1980s, laying the foundations for contemporary education and labour market conditions. Changes that were already evident in the early 1970s escalated during this period: the employment landscape for young people changed radically, and political responses took on new, harsher forms as the neo-liberal project gained momentum, bringing in its wake fresh 'civilising offensives' (Mennell 2015) against young people.

As Elias would remind us, sociological approaches that lack a historical grounding are, inevitably, deficient, and it is clear that an adequate understanding of the contemporary youth labour market cannot be achieved without an appreciation of changes taking place over several decades. The 1980s, as we have already seen, was a period of severe recession and political repositioning; many of the current issues relating to youth employment and unemployment can be traced back to this period. Indeed, the beginnings of what we now view as a crisis in youth unemployment in the 1980s were starting to emerge as early as the 1960s when, in some parts of the country, the early consequences of large-scale industrial decline began to be felt by young people (Goodwin and O'Connor 2005). These trends have led us to question the extent to which the growth of insecure and fragmented employment for young people is a recent phenomenon.

In this chapter, we develop our argument that the experience of young people in the 1980s can be seen as a key starting point for where we are now. We begin by demonstrating how many of the contemporary debates around current youth unemployment have their roots firmly in the 1980s crisis. For example, the punitive turn of the state towards young people, the focus on blaming certain groups of young people for their predicament (teenage mothers; black, Asian and ethnic minority youth; etc.), the threat of civil unrest, the rise of the 'under-class' and the labelling of young people as a 'lost generation' all emerged during this period.

The subsequent focus of this chapter is on the findings from secondary analy-sis of data relating to youth employment in the 1980s. Access to raw data in the form of two datasets collected in the early 1980s has allowed us to revisit the period with the benefit of hindsight to begin to identify the emergence of what have become longer-term trends in the youth labour market. Both studies formed the basis of important work in the 1980s by Ashton *et al.* (1986) and Roberts *et al.* (1986) and provided an insight into the experience of unemployment during this decade.

## The punitive turn

Young people leaving school in the late 1970s were the first cohort of the post-war period to experience, en masse, what has now become normalised for young people: a protracted, insecure and multi-step entry into the youth labour market and adult life alongside what Wacquant refers to as the 'gradual retrenchment of the social welfare' (2008: 80). The use of the term 'lost generation' to describe unemployed young people has its roots in this period of history (O'Higgins 2001; Nilsen and Brannen 2014).

During the 1980s, politicians warned of the consequences of long-term unemployment for young people leaving school during the recession. The *Times* (7 October 1981: 8), reporting on the Social Democratic Party (SDP)[1] conference in October 1981, used the headline 'Lost generation of young jobless could live to haunt society for years', in an article that quoted from the SDP leader Shirley Williams' opening speech:

> The children born in the bulge years of the late 50s and early 60s are the children who have been losers all along the lines. They went to overcrowded schools, saw their chances of an apprenticeship or a college place savagely cut, and are now moving in to a labour market which cannot offer them jobs. They are in danger of becoming a lost generation.

This narrative of a lost and forgotten generation positions young people as being 'victims' of the economic situation and demonstrates a largely support-ive and sympathetic approach to understanding the predicament of young people.

However, this period also saw the emergence of what we now know was the coming of a punitive[2] turn. Young people were increasingly demonised and blamed for their seeming inability to secure employment. Clarke and Willis noted this tendency in the early 1980s:

> the predominant focus of commentary and explanation [on youth unemployment] has been on the young people and implicitly, young, working-class people, as the problem. Equally, government initiatives aimed at 'solving' this problem have also focused on youth and their failings.
>
> (1984: 1)

Davies, writing in the *Guardian*, argued that planned changes to government policy, such as the removal of unemployment benefits, were evidence that young people were being 'threatened with a particularly punitive mix of coercion and poverty for a further year beyond the compulsory school leaving age' (1982: 9). He described the Youth Training Scheme (YTS) as 'new forms of training [that] are at root deeply pessimistic, preoccupied with the failures and weaknesses of youth and are based on a deficiency model of the young' (1982: 9).

A good example of the way in which the punitive turn began to emerge is found in the debates around the allowances young people would be paid for participating in YTS. One of the most contested suggestions of the period related to the planned withdrawal of the right of young people to claim supplementary benefit ('the dole') if they did not take up a place on the YTS. In June 1982, the then Employment Secretary, Norman Tebbit, announced that young people who were unemployed but refused to register for the schemes would not, as planned, have their benefits withdrawn, but 'teenagers who unreasonably refused a suitable training place would, like adults, have their benefit reduced for six weeks' (*Guardian* 22 June 1982: 21). Tebbit elaborated further on this point:

> I still believe that the Government's view of social security benefit for youngsters is the socially and morally correct one: to have an incentive to go on to constructive paths rather than an incentive to opt out.

Young people began to be accused of creating problems of unemployment themselves, and were criticised by employers for being unprepared for the world of work and for being 'unreliable and irresponsible' (*Guardian* 19 December 1983). The Youth Opportunities Programme (YOP) and YTS were positioned by the government as being, in part, about improving young people's employability rather than providing jobs, thereby subtly shifting the emphasis of blame from the economic situation and onto young people themselves.

The move towards apportioning blame on unemployed young people was visible from the early 1980s and set the scene for what was to come. In recent times, commentators such as Tyler (2013: 6.1) have argued that the concept of a 'deficit model' and the creation of an 'underclass' stem from New Labour policies of the late 1990s which 'systematically re-scripted problems of economic inequality and stagnant social mobility into matters of individual aspiration, will and choice'. However, we argue that this punitive turn actually began far earlier and can be traced back to the early 1980s, when the previously sympathetic tone shifted to one of blame as economic problems became increasingly entrenched. This was underpinned by changing policies that became less about supporting young people and more about penalising them.

The public face of this more punitive approach demonised particular groups of young people more than others. Black and Asian youth suffered significant racism and discrimination and, as a consequence, were less likely to secure employment or quality training places than their white counterparts (Hollands 1990). Teenage mothers also became victims of a growing blame culture:

> [There is] a kind of subdued moral panic simmering under the surface about young, unemployed girls becoming pregnant, staying single, and taking themselves out of the labour market by opting for full-time motherhood. These girls become dependant on welfare benefits rather than on a male breadwinner and it is this which has caused stories to surface in the tabloids about girls jumping the housing queues by getting pregnant, or by using pregnancy to get extra 'handouts'.
>
> (McRobbie 1989: 17)

A particular fear of the government focused on the perceived threat of civil unrest as a direct consequence of high and rising levels of unemployment in the early 1980s. In July 1980, the *Times* reported that

> [T]he Labour group's spokesman on Education repeated a warning that Britain was sitting on a time bomb; companies were closing, jobs were disappearing and the young unemployed were turning to drink, drugs, theft and violent crime.

A remarkably similar discourse was also evident in 2011:

> Youth unemployment will fuel disorder on the streets as disaffected teenagers are starved of hope for the future, the former Commissioner of the Metropolitan Police has warned. 'Looking ahead you can see there is disquiet on the streets [I'm] really concerned about youth unemployment, unemployment generally; really concerned about signs of an increase in crime'.
>
> (*Daily Telegraph* Online 6 December 2011)

Both of these articles, written some 30 years apart, also allude to the role of the family in creating problems of unemployment. The 1980s article quotes a Conservative spokesman who places the blame for the closure of firms on the parents of the young unemployed. Thirty years later, the perception that there are young people who have been brought up in homes where three generations are presumed to never have worked holds great currency among politicians, yet there is little evidence to support these claims (Shildrick *et al.* 2012).

The myths and stories created around the causes and consequences of youth unemployment in this period of recession have proved to be remarkably persistent and have been revisited and recreated in popular discourse during the more recent economic downturn. These myths perpetuate the idea that youth unemployment is largely explained by the individualised deficiencies of young people, thereby drawing attention away from economic causes and the lack of effective remedies through policy interventions.

## Revisiting the 1980s: zones of (in)security

The collapse of the youth labour market and concerns about the impact of the recession on young people's transitions from school to work led to increased research attention on the plight of young people living through these changes. With earlier research on transitions from school to work having taken place when the youth labour market was thriving, the new condition of youth raised great concern among researchers and policy makers. Teams led by both Ashton (1986) and Roberts *et al.* (1986) were funded by the Department of Employment to explore changes to the youth labour market as a consequence of the economic downturn. The data used in this chapter are derived from a secondary analysis of data collected for these two studies: Ashton's Young Adults project carried out in four contrasting labour markets (Leicester, Sunderland, St Albans and Stafford) in 1982–3, and Roberts's Changing Structure of Youth Labour Markets carried out in Liverpool, Walsall and Chelmsford in 1985.

The original project teams focused their attention on local labour markets to 'offer insights in to the main variations behind the prevailing national picture' (Roberts *et al.* 1986: 2) and to 'represent different local labour market conditions' (Ashton *et al.* 1986: 15). The specific local conditions ranged from those evident in the more prosperous, affluent towns of Chelmsford and St Albans, which offered opportunities for young people, to Walsall, Stafford and Leicester, each in a period of industrial change and decline and suffering increasing youth unemployment, through to Sunderland and Liverpool, which, as economically depressed cities, offered very few employment opportunities to school leavers.

For the purposes of our analysis we have combined the datasets and categorised these seven labour markets into three broad groups:

- Depressed: Sunderland and Liverpool (n = 874);
- Declining: Walsall, Leicester and Stafford (n = 870);
- Prosperous: St Albans and Chelmsford (n = 874).

This typology was not constructed to provide a robust geographical comparison, but as a starting point to enable a comparison with national-level data for the *c.* 2010s that can be found in the UK Household Longitudinal Study (*Understanding Society*), which is explored in Chapter 5. Such typologies are important, as they enable us to go beyond the national broad-brush picture to explore the variations in experience brought about by more local labour market conditions. As Ashton and colleagues suggest,

> if local labour markets have an effect on behaviour independently of other factors such as type of job, social background etc. then the use of large, nationally-representative samples as a basis of research are likely to miss these effects … [and do not] reflect the full range of factors operating at the local level.
>
> (1986: 105)

Neither of these datasets have previously been subject to secondary analysis. Yet, the re-analysis of this historic data has significant analytical value, as applying a contemporary conceptual lens that is more sensitive to the complexity of modern labour market experiences can offer significant new insights into changes taking place in the period. For example, the practice of conceptualising labour market position as a dichotomy between employment and unemployment (as reflected in the original analyses of these historic datasets) has been superseded, and there is now a far greater appreciation of the 'shades of grey' increasingly occupied by young people who are neither in full-time employment with stable contracts nor registered as unemployed.

Following the publication of Standing's book *The Precariat* (2011), the concept of 'precarity' has become widely used a means of understanding labour insecurity, although it has a longer pedigree in French sociology. As we argue in later chapters, the Precariat is a term that over-simplifies a more complex set of positions. In the 1980s, there was also a tendency to simply define young people's labour market status somewhat more starkly, as employed or unemployed. Much of the interest was in what was seen as an unprecedented level of youth unemployment and in understanding the experience of unemployed youth in contrast to that of the employed.

As Roberts (2010: 22) later argued, the categorisation of young people as employed/unemployed or 'sinkers and swimmers' (Wallace 1987) served to 'exemplify how dualistic language permeates youth transitions discourses', which, in turn, often neglects those in the middle. Similarly, by reducing our understanding of the youth labour market to dualisms we risk missing or underplaying the 'shades of grey' that were actually evident in the 1980s: part-time work, government training schemes, temporary or insecure work, zero hours contracts, unregistered unemployment.

Building on contemporary approaches to understanding the labour market, which go beyond dualisms in an attempt to capture non-traditional forms of employment, we created a new typology to retro-fit data from the two 1980s studies (Table 3.1). Here, informed by parallel analysis of the contemporary data reported in Chapter 5, the new categories have been framed to recognise what we refer to as 'zones of (in)security', supporting our argument that young workers in the 1980s can be understood, retrospectively, to have been among a new wave of workers in the post-war period to occupy non-traditional and insecure positions.

The three zones of (in)security we developed to understand the emerging features of the youth labour market can be termed the marginalised zone, the liminal zone and the traditional zone. Here (and in subsequent chapters focusing on the contemporary labour market), we describe these categories and explain how and why these zones provide a more accurate understanding of

*Table 3.1* Derived (in)security variable

| Marginalised zone | Liminal zone | Traditional zone |
| --- | --- | --- |
| • unemployed (unemployed, but working* + registered unemployed + unemployed, but not registered)<br>• workless (full-time students, maternity leave, looking after someone at home, long-term sick/disabled)<br>• part-time work: <= 10** hours pw<br>• 'fill-in' work<br>• government scheme<br><br>N = 1,126<br>(43%) | • part-time work: >10** hours pw<br>• self-employed<br>• temporary/insecure full-time work<br><br><br><br><br>N = 305<br>(12%) | • permanent/secure full-time work<br><br><br><br><br><br><br>N = 1183<br>(45%) |

* Unemployed and working describes those who are registered as unemployed but doing some work 'on the side'.
** The 1980s data were collected in such a way that part-time working could only be presented as less than and more than 10 hours.

change than one based on a new dichotomy: the precariat versus seemingly secure workers.

The traditional zone is made up of those individuals we regarded as 'traditional employees' from the interview schedules, being defined as those working in permanent, full-time jobs that they regarded as reasonably secure. This group accounted for nearly half (45 per cent) of the sample. The second category, the 'liminal zone', is occupied by just over one in ten respondents (12 per cent), including young people who, for various reasons, did not fit the traditional secure model of employment; specifically, those who were

- employed but in temporary or insecure full-time employment
- self-employed
- part-time (working for less than 30 hours but more than 10 hours per week).

The third category, the 'marginalised zone', accounted for just over four in ten respondents (43 per cent) who were in the most disadvantaged labour market positions; specifically, those who were

- on government schemes
- working in 'fill-in jobs'
- unemployed but working[3]
- registered unemployed
- unregistered unemployed
- workless (not in the labour market at the time of the interview).

These zones are represented in Figure 3.1, clearly depicting a liminal zone in the 1980s as a relatively small but significant zone of 'in-betweenness', comprising those young people who, at the time of interview, did not neatly fit 'positions assigned and arrayed' (Turner 1969: 95) in other studies of youth labour markets and whose status has all too often not been fully understood.

Clearly, in these 1980s studies the largest zone, by a very narrow margin, is the traditional zone. There is always a risk in the field of youth studies of focusing too much attention on the spectacular experiences and the 'extreme' cases. Much existing work is concerned with those on the margins, and in studies of the 1980s the focus has tended towards the problems of unemployment. This, coupled with media representations of the 1980s, puts us in danger of having a somewhat skewed vision of the past and over-emphasising problematic or non-linear transitions at the expense of the more successful, 'traditional' transitions from school to employment.

The danger in privileging complex transitions in youth research is that we may miss details of the lives of those experiencing the more 'ordinary' and

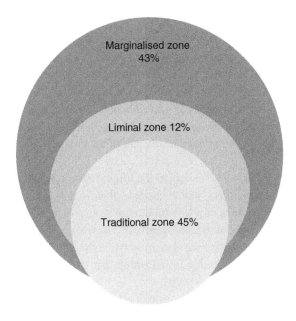

*Figure 3.1* Zones of (in)security (1980s)

unexceptional transitions to adulthood. This hazard of youth research was acknowledged in the 1980s, exemplified by Brown's study, *Schooling Ordinary Kids*, and his widely quoted description of this group of young people, 'who neither left their names engraved on the school honours board, nor gouged them into the top of classroom desks' (1987: 1). More recently, there has been a reigniting of interest in 'ordinary youth' at a time when much youth research has been characterised by research with young people situated on the margins of society and, possibly, at risk of becoming excluded or disconnected from it (Roberts and MacDonald 2013: 1.1). While we would not wish to downplay the unprecedented circumstances that 1980s school leavers found themselves in, there were, nonetheless, many who secured employment relatively quickly. As Roberts *et al.* (1986: 96) argued at the time: 'traditional transitions from school straight in to jobs … have not become extinct'.

The third zone, the marginalised zone, is fractionally smaller than the traditional zone but does clearly show the decimation of the youth labour markets in some of the areas covered by the two 1980s studies. Those in this zone were unemployed, workless or in 'fill-in jobs' and had been unable to secure traditional employment. Young people from the depressed and declining labour markets dominated this zone and had the lowest prospect of being able to transition from this zone into either a liminal or traditional position.

## Inside zones of (in)security

Using the zones of (in)security and the different labour market types as a basis for a secondary analysis of the combined datasets, we are able to cast more light on the complexities of the structure of the 1980s youth labour market. Of those who had secured jobs in the traditional zone, more than four in ten lived in one of the prosperous labour markets, while just over one in five lived in one of the depressed labour markets (Table 3.2). Conversely, while one in five young people in the marginalised zone lived in a prosperous labour market, nearly half of the group lived in a depressed labour market.

Perhaps surprisingly, the population who occupied the liminal zone tended to live in the more prosperous labour markets, which suggests that, in a period of national recession, different opportunities of a less traditional nature were opening up in the more buoyant, service-orientated labour markets. The two prosperous labour markets, St Albans and Chelmsford, were also areas with relatively strong service economies and, therefore, this provides an indication that the growth of liminality accompanied the growth of service sectors.

An analysis by gender shows that, within the marginalised zone, women were far more likely to be found in the workless category than men; but they were less likely to be registered unemployed, and more likely to be working part-time. These effects were found across all labour market types, suggesting that they were not due to local conditions and can be explained in other ways. The workless category, for example, includes women on maternity leave and those who were out of the labour market because they had dependent children. This mainly impacted on the Young Adults dataset which, with a higher age profile, had a far higher proportion of women with dependent children.

The over-representation of women among part-time workers can be explained by employment practices and conventions that were prevalent in the 1980s. Women with children frequently returned to work on a part-time basis, while employers often regarded part-time jobs as 'women's work'. Moreover, the 1980s saw the introduction of more flexible employment practices that suited the needs of employers seeking cost-cutting mechanisms. Among the respondents to the

*Table 3.2* (In)security by labour market type (%)

|                    |            | Zones of (in)security | | |
|--------------------|------------|-------------|---------|--------------|
|                    |            | *Traditional* | *Liminal* | *Marginalised* |
| **Labour markets** | **Prosperous** | 44 | 42 | 20 |
|                    | **Declining**  | 34 | 31 | 33 |
|                    | **Depressed**  | 22 | 27 | 47 |
| **Total**          |            | 100 | 100 | 100 |

1980s surveys, women were also strongly over-represented in the liminal zone, which itself was skewed towards part-time, rather than temporary or contract, workers.

In the 1980s, as today, educational qualifications were key to our understanding of young people's labour market experiences. As highlighted in the previous chapter, during the period preceding the recession of the 1980s the majority of young people, particularly in areas dominated by manufacturing industry, left school with few or no qualifications and secured low-skilled, but often relatively well-paid, employment in local factories. Ashton and Field's (1976) analysis of school to work transitions, illustrated in Chapter 2, showed clearly how young people's school and post-school pathways were largely pre-determined by their social class and their educational experiences. While some of the higher achieving young people from working-class families were able to secure apprenticeships and routine office-based roles, the majority entered semi- or unskilled manual jobs in the local labour market. Thus, in labour markets with a traditional manufacturing base, the post-war period was characterised by buoyant labour markets where employers did not have any expectation that young people would hold qualifications on leaving school.

In these areas, employment opportunities for unqualified school leavers were plentiful, and young people could be reasonably confident that even without formal qualifications they would secure jobs relatively easily (Furlong and Cartmel 1997). In contrast, opportunities in some of the more prosperous labour markets were increasingly skewed towards service-sector jobs with openings for white-collar, clerical and office-based jobs that commonly required school leavers to have some educational qualifications.

Data from the 1980s surveys show the extent to which young people in the more prosperous labour markets were investing in qualifications, while those living in the depressed labour markets had maintained a more traditional qualification profile in which far fewer had high-level qualifications. Of course, the social class profile of respondents makes the picture more complex, as the depressed cities of Liverpool and Sunderland had larger working-class communities than St Albans or Chelmsford. The surveys show clear differences in the average qualification profiles of young people in the different labour markets. Of those who had gained some A levels, 46 per cent lived in the more prosperous labour markets, but less than three in ten (29 per cent) in depressed labour markets. Of those with no qualifications, around half (51 per cent) lived in depressed labour markets but just one in five (19 per cent) in prosperous labour markets.

These data provide an insight into the increasing relevance of human capital for young people in the 1980s in some areas, with young people being aware of the pressure to obtain educational qualifications to be better prepared to enter the labour market. At the same time, they were caught in a paradoxical situation: in depressed labour markets, holding qualifications made very little difference to employers who were either not hiring young people or did not demand qualifications. As one respondent in Hollands' (1990: 31) study succinctly described,

> 'It's a vicious circle really 'cos they say yuh gotta work towards qualifications to get a job. Then you see the real world outside and there's no jobs around so you think I'm not doin' this anymore. So you drop out and then you do find that if you have qualifications it's an advantage, not much, but it is an advantage. But you can't work towards that advantage 'cos it's too late'.

Studies from this period (e.g. Ashton *et al.* 1986) show evidence of the disruption 'of time honoured patterns of social reproduction' (Tomlinson 2013: 7), whereby the jobs that had been held by the parents of these 1980s school leavers were disappearing fast and were not being replaced, leaving this generation as the first to face what was becoming a less secure and more unpredictable labour market.

This leads us to ask how far qualifications gained by young people in the early 1980s served to offer protection from poor labour market outcomes in the form of a route 'out' to more successful transitions. Were outcomes more dependent on labour market conditions than educational qualifications? What we find is that local labour market conditions do play a key role in determining outcomes. In the prosperous areas, securing educational qualifications was worthwhile because there, the entry level white-collar jobs required applicants to have qualifications. In the depressed areas, such as Sunderland, qualifications offered little protection against unemployment, as entry-level jobs were virtually non-existent.

In Ashton and colleagues' (1986) original analysis, they concluded that, even controlling for social background, young people in St Albans were achieving higher educational qualifications than young people in Sunderland. In combining both datasets, this pattern emerges even more markedly – young people in the prosperous labour markets achieved far higher qualifications than those in the declining or depressed areas. Ashton concluded that, although social class remained as significant in the 1980s as it had been in the 1960s, 'the virtual collapse of some industries has ... almost severed the relationships between social origins, school experience and the type of work entered that were characteristic of the 1960s and 1970s'. Of particular significance, here, is that Ashton extended this argument to suggest that 'local pockets of long term unemployment appear to be creating a new underclass, the children of which are further handicapped by their poor employment prospects' (1986: 32).

*Table 3.3* Qualifications gained by labour market types and zones of (in)security

| | Zones of (in)security | | |
| | Traditional | Liminal | Marginalised |
|---|---|---|---|
| **Prosperous labour markets** | | | |
| No qualifications | 44 | 8 | 48 |
| CSEs | 50 | 20 | 29 |
| O levels | 68 | 12 | 19 |
| A levels | 47 | 23 | 29 |
| **Depressed labour markets** | | | |
| No qualifications | 21 | 10 | 69 |
| CSEs | 19 | 8 | 73 |
| O levels | 44 | 11 | 44 |
| A levels | 37 | 8 | 55 |

Looking at the association between qualifications and labour market outcomes (Table 3.3), it is clear that the protection against marginalisation offered by qualifications is strongly conditioned by labour market conditions. In the more prosperous labour markets, nearly half (48 per cent) of those with no qualifications and nearly one in three with a Certificate of Secondary Education (29 per cent) were in the marginalised zone when interviewed; the corresponding figures for those living in depressed labour markets were significantly higher: 69 per cent and 73 per cent, respectively. In prosperous labour markets, nearly seven in ten (68 per cent) young people who gained O levels were in traditional forms of employment, compared to just over four in ten (44 per cent) in depressed labour markets. In both labour market types, qualifications conferred advantages, but their overall purchasing power was strongly conditioned by local conditions.

There was very little discernible difference between males and females across the labour market types. We found no statistically significant differences in the distribution of males and females in either the depressed or declining labour markets. However, in the prosperous labour markets females did tend to occupy the more disadvantaged positions. In these areas, more males than females were in the traditional zone (63.3 per cent vs 55.6 per cent), while this was reversed for the marginalised zone (22.3 per cent vs 29.6 per cent). This over-representation of women in the marginalised zone is explained, in part, by absence from the labour market due to motherhood, but it is more difficult to explain why this only occurred in the prosperous labour markets. Perhaps the explanation lies in the ubiquity of disadvantage in other labour markets in this period of time.

Roberts and colleagues (1987: 134) suggest that although job seekers in prosperous areas tended to be better qualified, some actually found it as hard to secure direct entry to jobs as did well-qualified job seekers in depressed and declining areas. They found, for example, that 'the best-qualified girls seemed to have the best job prospects not in Chelmsford but in Walsall and Liverpool' (p. 134). This was due to the type of employment available in each labour market and a reluctance among the young women to accept jobs for which they were over-qualified. Given that they were operating in a prosperous labour market with job opportunities available, there was little risk attached to spending a period of time out of work.

## Mobilities

So far, we have focused on the circumstances of respondents at the time they were interviewed. However, employment histories were also collected, which allows some analysis of changes of status over time; between first job and current job or between first status on leaving school and status at the time of interview. Beginning with first post-school destinations, we again find that labour markets are highly significant predictors of initial status. Whereas 46 per cent of those who moved straight from school to employment lived in prosperous labour markets, just 17 per cent of those following this trajectory lived in depressed labour markets (Table 3.4). Unemployment and government schemes were common first destinations for those living in declining and depressed labour markets, but much less common in prosperous areas.

Focusing on changes between first destination and status at time of interview (Figure 3.2), overall just over one in two respondents whose first labour market position was 'traditional' full-time employment had remained in such roles: in other words, what appeared on the surface to be a 'good start', as indicated by rapid movement to full-time work, turns out to be relatively insecure, as nearly half had moved to liminal or marginalised positions. Moreover, the overall picture hides variation by labour market. In the prosperous labour markets, the net move was from insecure to secure zones, with greater numbers in full-time jobs at time two than at time one. In the depressed and declining labour markets, movement towards the less secure zones was pronounced.

With government schemes in the 1980s frequently portrayed as dead-end destinations (Mizen 1990), an experience that did little to improve job prospects, our

*Table 3.4* First labour market status by labour market type (%)

|  | First labour market status | | | | |
|  | Employed | Gov. scheme | Unemp. | Out of l. m. | Other |
|---|---|---|---|---|---|
| Prosperous | 46 | 22 | 18 | 19 | 38 |
| Declining | 36 | 35 | 28 | 63 | 36 |
| Depressed | 17 | 43 | 54 | 18 | 26 |
| Total | 99 | 100 | 100 | 100 | 100 |

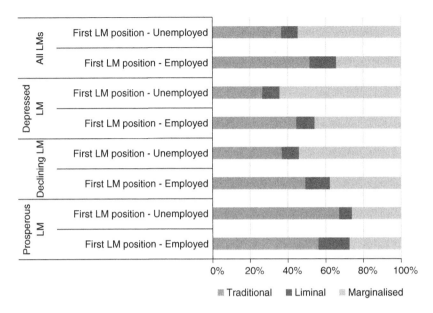

*Figure 3.2* First labour market status by zone of (in)security and labour market type (%)

data allow for further investigation of post-scheme destinations. Focusing on those whose first post-school destination was listed as a government scheme, in the prosperous labour markets nearly six in ten (58 per cent) listed their current destination as full-time employment (Figure 3.3). However, while schemes seemed to be relatively effective in buoyant labour markets, in the depressed labour markets just over one in five (22 per cent) had moved into full-time work, while more than one in two were subsequently unemployed. Interestingly, movement from schemes into insecure and temporary work or self-employment was much more common in the prosperous labour markets, again suggesting that those areas with strong service sectors were the first to witness a growth in non-standard employment opportunities.

Youth schemes were the first destination of more than one in ten respondents, a figure that is broadly in line with national participation rates on YTS in the early 1980s when these data were collected.[4] However, our data show clearly that the uptake of places varied widely according to local conditions and individual trajectories. For example, while just 13 per cent entered YTS as a first destination, this increases to 26 per cent when we consider the second labour market destination (reflecting the experience of school leavers who moved from education in to unemployment – first labour market status – and then moved on to a YTS scheme). Local-level data also show that scheme participation in the depressed labour markets (where participation was a majority experience) was double that found in the prosperous labour markets.

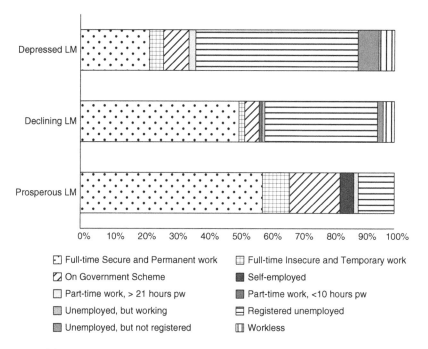

*Figure 3.3* Destination at time of interview of respondents whose first status was recorded as government scheme, by labour market type (%)

In both studies, the young people were asked to reflect on their experience of YTS. Respondents tended to provide mainly negative explanations for joining, such as being too young to claim unemployment benefit, rather than highlighting an expectation that training would lead to a secure job. Overall, perceptions of training schemes were, at best, ambivalent. However, where schemes were known to be 'good', which was usually defined as being well organised with clear learning and training outcomes, then the young people had far more positive views. Further, in the prosperous labour markets perceptions of training schemes were more positive; the young people were far less likely to attend multiple schemes, and there was a far higher probability that they would secure a job on completion of a single programme.

The experience of one of the young respondents in Liverpool illustrates some of the issues very effectively. After leaving school in May 1983, in August he began the first of a series of schemes. The first scheme, with a bookmaker, was described as 'no good' as it comprised 'menial tasks, mostly making tea. Not much to do with training'. By October, he was unemployed again and was signed up for a second training scheme in November. The second scheme included 2 weeks in a college plus block release and proved to be slightly more success-ful. However, during the course of the programme the employer moved to a new location which proved too far for the respondent to travel, leading to termination after 8 months. The subsequent period of unemployment lasted 6 months and ended with a job as a full-time sales assistant – a position which lasted for only 2 months, at the end of which the respondent was made redundant.

YTS was seen by this respondent and many others who took part in the research as a 'waste of time' or, as in this case, a 'load of rubbish' and an experience not worth repeating. This case is not untypical of experiences in the most depressed labour markets. With the benefit of hindsight, we can describe these experiences as illustrative of the labour market 'churning' that has been described in more contemporary labour markets (Furlong and Cartmel 2004; MacDonald and Marsh 1995). Indeed, the description of the experiences on YTS has remarkable resonance with contemporary descriptions of graduate internships which, it could be argued, operate largely as a type of YTS for unemployed graduates (O'Connor and Bodicoat, 2016).

The experiences of schemes and unemployment in this period are powerfully inter-linked, as illustrated by the previous example. Moreover, the long-term impacts of early unemployment on the future well-being of young adults are well known. Young people who experience poor outcomes in the transition from education to work and enter unemployment or temporary insecure work on leaving education are more likely to experience the long-term 'scarring effects' associated with early periods of insecurity. Bell and Blanchflower (2011: 260) have shown how scarring occurs in two ways: first, an early experience of unemployment 'raises the probability of being unemployed in later years', and second, such experiences also lead to a later wage penalty and lower earnings in future life.

Our data reveal that the local labour conditions were an important factor in determining the quality of early transitions, and, therefore, scarring is a process driven by labour market conditions. Here, two-thirds (67 per cent) of young people who were initially unemployed in the prosperous labour markets had moved into employment, whereas less than four in ten (37 per cent) of those in declining areas and less than three in ten (27 per cent) in the depressed areas had moved from unemployment to traditional employee roles.

In sum, young people living in prosperous areas were clearly privileged both in terms of initial destinations and in the likelihood of them moving from insecure positions into relatively secure forms of employment. The odds were stacked against those leaving school in the hardest-hit areas moving into secure employment, regardless of whether or not they participated on government schemes. In the depressed labour markets, qualifications provided some advantages, but were not a particularly good investment. In the areas most adversely affected by high levels of unemployment, school leavers were forced to adjust to the idea that there were few employment opportunities open to them. This was often reinforced by the advice provided by teachers and careers professionals, which increasingly and necessarily focused on how to navigate unemployment rather than providing advice on securing non-existent jobs. As one of Hollands' respondents put it,

> 'Everyone was sayin', everyone didn't think we'd get a job. Everyone thought we'd go straight on the dole … Yuh had a career lesson, listen, yuh had a career lesson, instead of talkin' about jobs, they talk about how to sign on the dole'.
>
> (1990: 38–9)

The unprecedented rise in youth unemployment in the early 1980s began to take on more significance as it became clear that this had become a long-term problem. Young people who had left school and failed to find work in the early part of the decade struggled to reverse their fortunes in challenging economic circumstances, and concerns were raised about the future prospects of this 'lost generation'. In 1983, the *Times* reported that not only were there gaps in provision for young people, but recurrent spells of unemployment were affecting many:

> Long-term unemployment among a 'forgotten generation' is pointing to a wide gap in the provisions […]. More than 410,000 of those aged 18–25 have been out of work for more than a year … Recurrent spells of unemployment are a serious difficulty for a significant group among the unemployed.
>
> (*Times* 21 July 1983)

As Ashton and colleagues had concluded, the local labour market 'was important in determining the young persons' chances of entering full-time work … and the likelihood of becoming and remaining for long periods unemployed' (1986: 104). Among those in depressed and declining labour markets, the threat of long-term unemployment had started to become a reality. As we have shown, young people in the depressed labour markets were most likely to leave school and begin their 'working lives' as unemployed and fared worst in the long run. These areas were particularly hard hit by the decline in the manufacturing industry and the disappearance of manual jobs that previously provided routes into work for young, unqualified and unskilled school leavers (McDowell 2003). Our data show that the impact of these changes to the manufacturing base in the hardest hit regions, which impacted on men and women alike, had serious consequences.

## Psychological well-being

Historically, researchers have paid little attention to either the physical health or the psychological well-being of young people. As West argues in relation to physical health, 'twenty years ago, the health of young people barely featured on the social health and policy agendas… (re)affirming a widespread but fallacious assumption that youth and health go hand in hand' (2009: 331). Yet, recent research has shown that young people are increasingly likely to suffer from poor health, both physical and psychological, which can be linked to broader socioeconomic changes (Eckersley 2009). Indeed, Bell and Blanchflower (2011), using data from the 1958 National Child Development Study birth cohort study, have highlighted the negative long-term impacts of early experiences of unemployment on measures including life satisfaction, health status, mental health and job satisfaction.

Undoubtedly, adverse circumstances, such as long periods of unemployment, can have a significant impact on mental health, and the potential consequences of unemployment on the psychological well-being of young people was beginning to be recognised in the 1980s. Both Ashton and colleagues (1986) and Roberts and colleagues (1987) included questions about respondents' subjective feelings about unemployment in their studies. While not focused explicitly on psychological well-being and mental health, these questions were intended to help the researchers understand the individual experience of unemployment and recession.

Lack of money and boredom were significant issues, and many respondents mentioned the difficulties of finding work and worry about future prospects as being problematic aspects of unemployment. An interesting geographical disparity found by Ashton and colleagues was that the negative impact of the difficulty experienced in finding work was more pronounced among young people in one of the declining labour markets (Stafford) than in the depressed labour market of Sunderland. This finding, they suggest, may have reflected the acceptance of the futility of seeking work in a depressed labour market. This sense of an adjustment by young people being made to local labour market conditions is reinforced by the findings of Banks and Ullah (1988), who reported that it proved difficult to identify a simple relationship between length of unemployment and psychological well-being of young people in the 1980s. This, they argue, suggests that 'some form of adjustment to unemployment has been made, even though … the young unemployed report significantly more psychological distress than their employed counterparts' (1988: 151).

The idea of young people having to adjust psychologically to an increasingly challenging labour market is further supported by their finding that young people who left school at the start of the recession (1981) were more adversely affected by the experience of unemployment than the later school leavers. This suggests that the younger group of school leavers had lower expectations of the labour market, having been exposed to the widely publicised experience of earlier leavers, and there had 'possibly … been a collective adjustment to poor employment prospects' (p. 70).

With a wide range of contemporary studies now showing clear linkages between young people's labour market experiences and patterns of psychological malaise, we can probably assume that, although lacking visibility, labour market conditions in the 1980s took a toll on the mental health and well-being of those young people entering the labour market in this era. Indeed, Rutter and Smith (1995) have argued that psycho-social disorders among young people have been increasing since the 1970s (perhaps earlier) and suggest that there is a clear association between unemployment and psychological disorders, depression, anxiety and self-esteem as well as reductions in happiness and life satisfaction.

## Conclusion

The 1980s was a watershed decade; some of the trends that were visible in the 1970s escalated and, under Margaret Thatcher, a neo-liberal agenda underpinned the policy response, which was transformed from one that was broadly sympathetic to the plight of youth to one that regarded young people with suspicion. While the immediate post-war decades represented what, in retrospect, was a boom period of youth employment (though not without some complexities (Goodwin and O'Connor 2005)), the 1980s saw in a spectacular rise in youth unemployment and a transformation of youth transitions which, with the rapid growth of schemes, meant that transitions for significant numbers of young people became multi-stage.

With the transition from school to work in the 1980s coming to be symbolised by two key themes – high levels of youth unemployment and YTS – we must be mindful that, while young people in some areas suffered extremely badly, others were minimally affected. Indeed, our academic preoccupation with the 1980s as a time of 'spectacular' youth transitions has meant that the ordinary youth of this period have often been ignored, and it is easy to forget that many young people continued to make one-step transitions into what we have termed the traditional zone. These transitions were certainly mediated by geography, class, gender and ethnicity, yet what we have seen from the 1980s data is that the origins of the current experiences of young people, so widely discussed by academics, policy makers, politicians and the media, can, as this chapter has shown, be traced back to this era. In this chapter, we have suggested that non-standard forms of employment began to increase in the more prosperous areas, labour markets where the balance of opportunities was already skewed towards the service sector.

Almost 40 years on, it is evident that the changes brought about by industrial decline, coupled with the increasing numbers of young people entering higher and further education, tightened benefit regulations and increasing levels of government intervention were already beginning in the 1980s. What we are witnessing now is, to some extent, simply an extension of what began almost four decades ago; the short-term, temporary and insecure work that characterises the current recession was also in evidence for these young workers in the 1980s (Furlong and Cartmel 1997).

There is some evidence to suggest that, over time, the position of these 1980s school leavers improved, and there was movement between the zones of insecurity and traditional employment. However, this was mainly evident among young people who had the advantage of living in a prosperous labour market. Here, young people had begun to invest in education in the realisation that new opportunities required qualifications. The most vulnerable youth faced far more problematic transitions, particularly in the most disadvantaged labour markets. In these areas the opposite trends were apparent, and transitions into unemployment, insecurity and precarious work alongside government schemes were well on the way to becoming established trajectories for young people. As Ashton and colleagues (1986) suggested, the 1980s saw the emergence of a strata of insecure workers: 'of insecurities and fragmentation among those with the fewest cards to play in the job market' (Fenton and Dermott 2006: 219).

## Notes

1   The Social Democratic Party subsequently merged with the Liberal Party to become the Liberal Democrats.
2   What we refer to as the 'punitive turn' was marked by several pieces of legislation introduced in the early 1980s. See Mack and Lansley (1985).
3   In this era, unemployment benefit regulations were framed so that it was acceptable to work for a limited number of hours a week while remaining eligible for benefits.
4   The more widely quoted figure of one in four young people being engaged in YTS was not a reality until later in the decade (peaking in 1988–9 at 24 per cent (Deakin 1996)).

# Chapter 4

# Towards a new normality

## Work and unemployment in contemporary Britain

> The main issue in the current recession is the lack of demand. Unemployment has not risen because people have chosen to be unemployed. Unemployment is largely involuntary. The reserve army of the unemployed is a conscript army not a volunteer army. Unemployment makes people unhappy. It lowers the happiness of the people who are unemployed but also lowers the happiness of everyone else.
>
> (Bell and Blanchflower 2009)

## Introduction

In the previous two chapters, we largely focused on the period beginning in the 1960s and ending in the 1980s, examining changes in young people's experiences of work and the impact of the significant rise in youth unemployment in the early part of that decade. We argued that the election of Margaret Thatcher in 1979 and her government's embrace of a neo-liberal agenda led to significant changes in the ways in which the debate on youth (un)employment was framed, and the policies adopted, which set the scene for that decade and beyond.

Following the 1980s recession, unemployment rates did not return to pre-recession levels for 10 years (Spence 2011); rates peaked in 1984 and declined relatively steadily until a further recession in the early 1990s led to another upward turn. Young people's experiences from the 1980s onwards were shaped by the expansion of educational opportunities and by growing expectations regarding the length of participation. As a result, employment rates among young people continued to fall from the mid-1990s to the present day, especially among 16- and 17-year-olds. These changes in patterns of participation, and the associated rise in qualification profiles, had an impact on young people's expectations.

Job creation in the aftermath of the 1980s recession, and again following the 1990s recession, continued to involve a shift from the manufacturing to the service sector and involved a further loss of traditional apprenticeships and the introduction of what were referred to as 'modern apprenticeships'. With an increase in qualifications among young people and a decline in industrial employment, those leaving education at the minimum age with relatively poor credentials faced difficulties in times of growth as well as in times of contraction.

We begin this chapter by examining changes in employment opportunities from the early 1990s to the present day, looking at trends and highlighting the extent that different groups were affected by these changes. This is followed by a discussion of changing patterns of unemployment in the 1990s recession and the Great Recession and in their aftermath. Here, we also outline the new measures introduced to serve those experiencing unemployment and discuss the changing principles that underpin policy development.

## Changing structures of opportunity

Since the 1980s recession, governments in the United Kingdom and in other developed countries have encouraged increased participation in the upper secondary school and in tertiary education. These policies have been successful to the extent that there has been a more or less continual growth in educational participation and, across the Organisation for Economic Cooperation and Development (OECD) countries, very few young people now leave without completing upper secondary education. Higher education has also been transformed from an elite to a mass experience.

While national governments have often promoted increased educational participation on the grounds that a more educated population is believed to enhance economic competitiveness, from a young person's perspective an awareness that unqualified leavers have poor employment prospects has encouraged young people to take shelter in education: a discouraged worker effect.

In the United Kingdom, between 1984 and 2013, full-time educational participation among 16- to 24-year-olds increased from 1.42 million to 3.03 million (despite the fact that the overall youth population fell by a million over the same period) (ONS 2014). As a result, young people in the labour market in the Great Recession were better educated than in the previous two recessions: compared to 1993, the number of 16- to 24-year-olds who were graduates had doubled (Bell and Blanchflower 2009). Consequently, the number of young people in employment has fallen: whereas in 1992 nearly one in two 16- and 17-year-olds (48.4 per cent) were in employment, by 2011 less than one in four 16- and 17-year-olds (23.5 per cent) held any form of employment (Bivand *et al.* 2011; Spence 2011).

On a societal level, educational policies have helped limit unemployment by reducing the numbers of young people exposed to the labour market. On an individual level, time spent in education decreases the likelihood of unemployment and can open up economic and social horizons. As Bivand and colleagues (2011) note, employers primarily focus recruitment on young people with higher qualifications. Education is also linked to healthier lifestyles and a more positive sense of well-being (Baum *et al.* 2013).

> A college education does not carry a guarantee of a good life or even of financial security. But the evidence is overwhelming that for most people, education beyond high school is a prerequisite for a secure lifestyle and significantly improves the probabilities of employment and a stable career with a positive earnings trajectory. It also provides tools that help people to live healthier and more satisfying lives, to participate actively in civil society, and to create opportunities for their children.
>
> (Baum *et al.* 2013: 7)

While education provides advantages to the individual as well as benefits to the state in terms of reduced welfare benefits and increased tax revenues, on the negative side, the increase in qualified school and university leavers has fuelled a process of qualification inflation, making it much more difficult for qualified young people to enter high-skill positions. As a result, young people may incur significant debts without securing access to enhanced earnings or stimulating jobs.

Although young people today have better qualifications than they did in the 1980s or 1990s recessions, they are still heavily concentrated in low-skill sectors of the economy. Among 16- to 24-year-olds, more than seven in ten work in elementary occupations, such as waitressing and catering assistants, and sales and customer services (ONS 2014). With many young people in this age group being in full-time education, for some the jobs they hold will be regarded as temporary, and there will be an expectation of higher-skilled occupations on completing their education. If the occupational distribution is confined to those who have left full-time education, the range of jobs they hold is more varied, although still skewed towards the low-skilled occupations (Figure 4.1).

The overall distribution of jobs for young people has been shaped by the continued decline of the manufacturing sector (which declined by 17.2 per cent between 1979 and 2010) and the continued growth of the service sector (which grew by 21.5 per cent over the same period) (Spence 2011), which has tended to involve a growth of low-skill, low-pay occupations.

Indeed, drawing on information from the UK Labour Force Surveys from 1979 to 1999, Goos and Manning (2007) argued that trends showed a growth in what they referred to as 'lousy jobs' over 'lovely jobs'; lousy jobs being defined as those with low median wages such as care workers. Replicating Goos and Mannings' analysis for the years 2002 to 2008, Bell and Blanchflower (2009) found both a growth in 'lovely' jobs and a modest growth of 'lousy' jobs with a

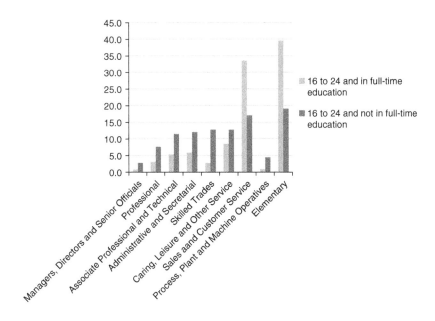

*Figure 4.1* The occupational distribution of young people (excluding students), United Kingdom, 2013

Source: Derived from figures presented in ONS 2014.

significant decline in jobs in the middle ranges (sometimes referred to as the hour-glass economy), as did Sissons (2011). Focusing on occupational change among 16- to 24-year-olds, Bell and Blanchflower (2009) also found a heavy concentration of young people in 'lousy' jobs in the lowest earnings decile.

In an economy where there are concentrations of opportunities at the top and bottom ends of the labour market and a shortage of jobs in the middle ranges, and where young people most frequently enter the labour market at the bottom end, there can be great difficulties in achieving the long-range mobility necessary to move from 'lousy' to 'lovely' jobs (Bell and Blanchflower 2009). Polarised opportunity structures can be difficult to traverse and may trap qualified young people in unskilled sectors of the economy.

This is a particularly vexed issue as we have an expansion of well-qualified young people, many of whom hold university degrees, in an economy where much expansion is at the lower end of the skill spectrum. In the post-recession United Kingdom, with political sensitivities about the extent to which austerity measures are helping promote economic growth, the government has been keen to highlight the creation of new jobs. At the same time, the Trades Union Congress (TUC) has shown that only six in ten new jobs are employee positions (the remainder involving self-employment, unpaid family work and so on), while three in ten new jobs are part-time (TUC 2013). Indeed, between summer 2010 and the end of 2012, nearly eight in ten new jobs were in low-paid industries[1] (77 per cent) (TUC 2013).

As a consequence, there has been an increase in the number of young people working in jobs for which they are over-qualified. Poor job prospects and qualification inflation have encouraged young people to remain in education in the hope that, in the long term, they can access interesting jobs in the more secure sectors of the labour market. Yet, the evidence shows that many graduates are failing to get a foothold in the graduate labour market. With an increase in the number of graduates without a corresponding increase in graduate jobs, it has been estimated that the United Kingdom will have a surplus of at least 50,000 graduates a year (Birchall 2009).

In the United Kingdom, figures from the Labour Force Survey show that only a quarter of graduates earned more than the overall average, while a similar proportion received below average wages (Byrnin 2013). In the United Kingdom 6 months after graduation, at least four in ten graduates are in low-skill forms of employment, and 3.5 years after graduation one in four remain in low-skill jobs (Mosca and Wright 2011).

The expansion of part-time employment among young people has fuelled a growth in underemployment under which employees who would like to work full time have little option but to accept part-time jobs. In the United Kingdom, as in much of Europe, there is concern about the rise in the number of young people holding part-time jobs, or even juggling a number of part-time jobs, when they would really like a full-time job. These young workers, who are more prevalent in the United Kingdom than the Organisation for Economic Cooperation and Development (OECD) average (Bell and Blanchflower 2009), are often overlooked in policy terms, and some struggle economically.

As we saw in Chapter 2, part-time working for young people, which was extremely rare in the 1960s and 1970s, started to become more common in the 1980s, although it remained a minority experience. However, during the 1990s there was a significant increase in part-time working among young people; in 1996, for example, three-quarters of those who found jobs during the winter went into part-time work. Walker, writing in 1997, argued that 'almost the entire net gain in employment since 1990 came from part-time jobs' (1997: 14).

Research by the TUC (2012) has shown that since the start of the recession, underemployment has increased by a million; an increase of 42 per cent. Moreover, they argue that young people are almost twice as likely to be underemployed, with one in five young people affected. Bell and Blanchflower (2013) compared the hours that people say they would like to be able to work with those they actually work; they estimate that in the United Kingdom, underemployment among 16- to 24-year-olds stands at 30 per cent. Figures from the Labour Force Survey between the first quarter of 2008 and the third quarter of 2009 show a fall of 4 per cent in hours worked among those in employment (Spence 2011).

Campbell (2015) uses the term 'time-related underemployment' to describe the increasingly prevalent phenomenon whereby people who wish for full-time jobs hold part-time jobs and are unable to secure the hours they need to secure the desired standard of living. Using figures from the Australian Labour Force Survey he shows that while, in 2015, unemployment among 15- to 24-year-olds stood at 12.9 per cent, underemployment had reached 16.1 per cent.

While there has been a long-running debate about whether young people's wage levels effectively price them out of the jobs market, Bell and Blanchflower (2009) suggest that much of the evidence is dated and comes from an era where trade unions had more influence on wage rates. Indeed, youth wages have been in decline for well over a decade, and there is a lack of contemporary data suggesting that young people's wage rates are pricing them out if the job market. Indeed, young people and older workers tend not to compete directly with each other for jobs, as 'young people are rarely seen as good substitutes for older workers (or vice versa) and the formal evidence, where it exists, tends to show that replacing one kind of worker with another, according to age, is limited' (O'Higgins 2001: 17).

## Trends in (un)employment

In the previous chapter, we commented on youth unemployment in the 1980s recession and its aftermath. After a peak of 1.25 million in the early 1980s, youth unemployment fell fairly sharply until the onset of the 1990s recession. The 1990s recession involved a much lower peak and a more rapid recovery (Bivand *et al.* 2011). While the years between the mid-1990s and the 2008–9 recession involved relatively low levels of youth unemployment, Bivand and colleagues point out that over the last two decades youth unemployment has never fallen below half a million and that a rise was evident well before the 2008–9 recession.

The period beginning in the mid-1980s and extending to the onset of the Great Recession has been referred to by economists as the 'Great Moderation' (Stock and Watson 2002). This period was characterised by a relative stability in business cycles involving low levels of volatility due to a lack of fiscal shocks and stable commodity prices. Gordon Brown referred to it as 'the end of the boom and bust economy' in which fluctuations in employment and unemployment rates were much reduced. However, while one would expect the 'Great Moderation' to provide employers with greater incentives to invest in human capital, over the period there was a growth in temporary and part-time employment (Ćorić 2011). One of the reasons for the growth in employment insecurity during a period when the economy lacked the levels of volatility that characterised the 1970s and early 1980s can be linked to the ongoing decline of manufacturing industry and the growth of the service sector. While modern manufacturing industry requires investment in task-specific skills, the service sector, with its demand for soft skills, may require less investment in skills and frequently has peaks and troughs in demand that steer employers towards part-time hours and flexible contracts.

This period of low volatility came to an abrupt end with the global shock waves linked to the sub-prime loan crisis in the United States and the collapse of institutions such as Lehman Brothers in the autumn of 2008. Young people below the age of 18 were most affected by the 2008–9 recession; whereas one in four were unemployed in the first quarter of 2008, in 2011 almost four in ten were unemployed. Over the same period, unemployment among 18- to 24-year-olds rose from just over 12 per cent to almost 18 per cent (Figure 4.2). The peaks in unemployment associated with the 2008–9 recession were very similar to those recorded in the 1980s recession (ONS 2014) and, unlike the 1990s recession, involved an upwards drift that continued well after the recession formally ended. As Bivand and colleagues argue, 'so far, for young people this recession has more in common with the 1980s, with a prolonged period of high unemployment and rising long-term unemployment' (2011: 4).

Long-term unemployment among young people has always been a cause for concern, and many activation programmes have specifically targeted those who have been unemployed for some time. While long-term youth unemployment among 16- to 24-year-olds fell from a peak of over a quarter of a million in the 1990s recession to a low of 55,000 in 2002, it had doubled (to 110,000 in 2007) immediately before the recession and continued to rise throughout the recession, crossing the quarter-million mark again in 2011 (Bivand *et al.* 2011). Around a

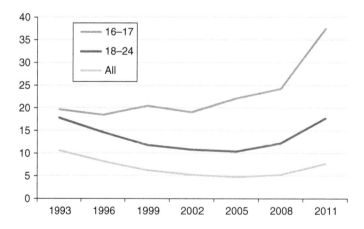

*Figure 4.2* Unemployment rates, by age

Source: Derived from figures collected by the Labour Force Survey (various).

quarter of young people who were unemployed at this time had been workless for over a year (Bivand *et al.* 2011).

Levels of youth unemployment, and particularly long-term unemployment, in the United Kingdom have remained stubbornly high in the post-recession environment; however, the same is true in other European countries. Overall, the United Kingdom falls slightly below the overall EU average for youth unemployment, although of course the average is strongly influenced by the extremes of several southern European countries. In 2013, in Greece and Spain almost six in ten young people were unemployed, compared to around one in five in the United Kingdom (Figure 4.3). In contrast, Germany and Austria had youth unemployment rates of less than 10 per cent, largely as a result of the maintenance of a strong system of vocational training and long-established apprenticeships set within a highly regulated labour market.

There are also strong regional variations in youth unemployment rates within the United Kingdom. With regional economies affected by their industrial make-up and susceptible in different ways to trade cycles and global economic trends, the historic surveys that we examined in Chapter 3 drew on regions that were differentially affected by the 1980s recession and, as a consequence, levels of youth unemployment covered a broad spectrum: ranging, among Roberts's 17- and 18-year-olds, from 41 per cent in Liverpool to 8 per cent in Chelmsford (Roberts *et al.* 1986). In 2013, one in five or more 16- to 24-year-olds were unemployed in the Northeast, West Midlands, Yorkshire and Humberside, Wales, Northern Ireland and London, unemployment rates were up to 10 percentage points lower in the East of England and the Southeast (ONS 2014) (Figure 4.4).

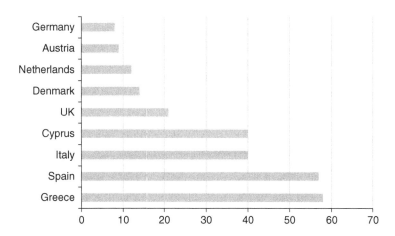

*Figure 4.3* Youth unemployment rates, 2013 (third quarter)

Source: Derived from Eurostat figures presented in ONS 2014.

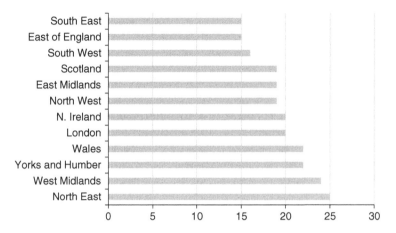

*Figure 4.4* Unemployment rates among 16- to 24-year-olds by region
Source: Derived from ONS 2014.

While labour market statistics provide a clear overview of trends and show the extent to which young people suffer through changing opportunity structures and economic upheavals, less visible are shifting interpretations of the causes and consequences of youth unemployment. In particular, throughout the 1990s the Thatcher legacy continued to colour both attitudes and policies towards the unemployed (especially young unemployed). Despite clear evidence that youth unemployment was primarily caused by a deficit in demand, by skill mismatches and by spatial unevenness in opportunities, politicians frequently suggested that young people were a major part of the problem. Indeed, what we referred to as the 'punitive turn', which was enshrined legislatively in the early 1980s, continued to shape unemployment policy through the 1990s and to the present day. Governed under a regime of intolerance, young people are increasingly 'subject to suspicion, scrutiny and assessment combined with compulsory divulgence and attendance, training and other exercises to become "job-ready" all backed up with threats of sanction' (Boland and Griffin 2015).

## The consequences of unemployment

While the psychological costs of unemployment are clearly documented, with strong evidence of a causal link between unemployment and psychological distress, reduced self-esteem and a decline in life satisfaction (e.g. Banks and Ullah 1988; West and Sweeting 1996), policy tends to be underpinned by a different set of assumptions. Here, young people are cast not as victims of circumstances largely beyond their control, but either as misguided individuals who have failed to take the appropriate steps to secure employment or as work-shy transgressors who are playing the system.

Interpretations that rest on a premise of deficient labour supply are the foundation upon which most work activation and skill development programmes are built. For that very reason, few are effective (Furlong and McNeish 2000). Throughout the 1990s, a number of new programmes were introduced. For young people the most significant landmarks were the introduction of Youth Training (YT) (launched in 1993 to replace the Youth Training Scheme (YTS)); Modern Apprenticeships and Accelerated Modern Apprenticeships (introduced in 1996) to cater, respectively, for 16- to 17-year-olds and 18- to 19-year-olds; and the New Deal for Young People (1998), targeting 18- to 24-year-olds unemployed for 6 months or more.

Each of these programmes placed an increased emphasis on skill development, while other trends involved contracting provision for the long-term unemployed out to the private and third sectors and a greater tendency to underpin provision with the threat of benefit sanctions for those who failed to participate. For example, Workwise, a 4-week intensive programme aimed at 18- to 24-year-olds who had been without work for a year, imposed a 40 per cent reduction in Income Support benefit for anyone failing to attend. Similarly, 1-2-1, a series of structured interviews for the same client group, was able to use full benefit suspension in the case of non-compliance.

YT (a re-packaged variant of YTS) guaranteed places for 16- to 17-year-olds, but, given the withdrawal of income support for most young people, it was only through accepting a placement that young people without a job had access to any form of financial support. YT aimed to provide better quality training than previous schemes and promised to significantly increase the numbers gaining level 2 and 3 qualifications. With an increased tendency for young people to complete upper secondary education, more places were provided for the 18-plus age group.

However, from the 1972 Training Opportunities Programme through its various incarnations, such as the Youth Opportunities Programme, the YTS and the New Deal for Young People, schemes for young people who encounter a period of unemployment have been continually criticised, mainly on account of low-quality training, poor job placement rates and a failure to convince young people of the alleged benefits of participation. YT was no exception. YT was criticised for failing to honour its guarantee to make places available to eligible 16- to 17-year-olds in a timely fashion as well as for a poor record in job placement and improved qualifications. Indeed, a survey conducted in 1995 showed that up to 60 per cent of young people who participated in the programme had no qualifications on leaving (*Independent* 1995).

Introduced under John Major's Conservative government, Modern Apprenticeships were another attempt to provide better quality training and to address a perceived deficit in technician and intermediate level qualifications. With the programme aimed at bringing 16- to 24-year-olds up to National Vocational Qualification (NVQ) level 3 qualifications, Fuller and Unwin have argued that 'the use of the term "apprenticeship" was a deliberate attempt to set the new programme aside from existing "youth training" schemes which had struggled to shake off an image of low quality' (2013: 8).

Comparing Modern Apprenticeships with German apprenticeships, Ryan and Unwin (2001) argued that Modern Apprenticeships came closer to YT than to the German model. They argued that in the UK programme, rates of completion were relatively poor, as was the breadth and depth of training. Given that Modern Apprenticeships were supposedly about upskilling to NVQ level 3, only one in two leavers attained that level of qualification. Acknowledging some improvement over time, Ryan and Unwin nevertheless argued that 'Modern Apprenticeship activity was biased towards short, low-cost programmes and skills not in short supply, particularly in the service sector' (2001: 108). While echoing concerns about the poor-quality training offered to many modern apprentices, Fuller and Unwin (2013) also voiced concerns about gender segregation. While the overall uptake between males and females was relatively balanced, industries such as health and social care and customer service were very heavily skewed towards females (86 per cent and 69 per cent, respectively), while engineering and construction were almost exclusively male (recruiting 3 per cent and 2 per cent females, respectively).

Modern Apprenticeships ran alongside YT rather than replacing it, with the former able to recruit young people with the strongest qualifications. While from the outset youth training schemes had always been stratified between high- and low-quality forms of delivery, Modern Apprenticeships took these divisions to a new level. As Maclagan argued, Modern Apprenticeships offer 'some young people high quality opportunities by implicitly devaluing or marginalising what is available for the less favoured' (1996: 16).

The New Deal for Young People, launched in 1998, was the flagship offering of the incoming Blair government. Upholding the workfare approach to benefits, the New Deal guaranteed a place for all young people who had been unemployed for 6 months and, following a period of assessment and tailored support through a personal advisor, offered the young person the (mandatory) 'option' of

- a subsidised job placement for up to 6 months;
- a place on a full-time course of education or training lasting up to 12 months;
- a work placement with the environmental task force for up to 6 months; or
- a work placement with the community task force lasting up to 6 months.

Those who refused one of these options were sanctioned by withdrawal of their jobseekers (unemployment) benefits, while those who participated were not paid a wage but received an allowance of the equivalent of jobseekers benefit. In addition, young people on the environment or community task forces received an extra £15 per week, while the employers of those undertaking job placements were provided with a subsidy of £60 per week as well as £750 to cover any training costs.

While some evaluations of the New Deal (e.g. Riley and Young 2000) were very positive, highlighting a significant reduction in long-term youth unemployment, others were less complimentary. Myck (2002), for example, argued that unemployment was falling anyway, and groups who were ineligible for the New Deal also experienced reduced unemployment. Others argued that while there was a reduction in long-term unemployment, which may or may not have been linked to the New Deal, as many as one in five of those who passed through the scheme entered jobs lasting less than 13 weeks, and a third of those participating in 2007 had past experience of the programme and were effectively being recycled (Bivand et al. 2011), offering the private sector fresh opportunities to profit from their failure to provide young people with high-level skills.

Launched in 2011, the current flagship scheme is the Work Programme. Contracted out to private and third sector organisations, the Work Programme operates on a payment by results basis which has led to accusations that, driven by the profit motive, providers are focusing on clients who are regarded as easiest to place while marginalising those with deep-seated issues. Like its predecessors, the Work Programme recruits participants under threat of loss of benefit, being mandatory for 18- to 24-year-olds who have been unemployed for 9 months.

The Work Programme has come in for much criticism due to its abysmal rates of job placement: in its first year of operation, of the 785,000 people who passed through the scheme, just 2.3 per cent subsequently held a job for 6 months or more (Murray 2012). Indeed, it has been argued that 'more people will have been sanctioned by the Work Programme than properly employed through it' (Richard Whittell, quoted in the *Guardian*, Boffey 30 June 2012).

## The jeopardisation of labour as the new normality

The period beginning in the early 1990s and extending to the present day has witnessed the acceleration of trends already evident in the 1970s and 1980s, such as the further decline in manufacturing industry and growth in services, and an increase in part-time and temporary forms of employment, set against the backdrop of an increasingly educated workforce. In the modern hourglass economy, opportunities are increasingly polarised.

While it is easy to put forward explanations for employment insecurity that focus on new patterns of demand and the ways in which employers seek to maintain or enhance profitability by finding novel ways of reducing wage costs, these interpretations are partial. In an economy dominated by a service sector where investment in hard skills is relatively low, it is easy to see how employers come to regard labour as a disposable commodity. Indeed, in the dog-eat-dog world of modern capitalism, labour conditions deteriorate as employers engage in a race to the bottom. Many of the so-called success stories of the modern service economy are ones that have attracted criticism for their employment policies and labour strategies; for example, Uber, Deliveroo, Hermes and Sports Direct.

Yet in all this, government has a role to play and has a responsibility for setting the framework in which firms compete. In the United Kingdom, as in many other advanced societies, governments of left, right and centre have largely accepted the new conditions and helped embed what Castel refers to as the 'jeopardization of labor', of which 'unemployment is only the most visible manifestation of a profound transformation in the larger state of employment' (2003: 380). For Castel, as well as for ourselves, the stratification between the 'protected sectors and vulnerable workers' (2003: 329) can be traced back to the early 1970s.

Through the various interventions that we have described in this and the preceding chapters, UK governments have been sensitive to the potential political fallout generated by high levels of youth unemployment, but they have never displayed the will to invest in high-quality training to provide the sort of workforce that will attract inwards investment by high-tech multinationals. Whereas Germany, Austria and Switzerland have maintained a high-quality system of apprenticeships, and while the Asian tiger economies, such as Singapore, have invested heavily in education and skill development, the United Kingdom has maintained what Ashton and colleagues have referred to as a 'low skill equilibrium': 'reinforcing a national system of training which is inappropriate for an advanced industrial society' (1990: 201).

The 'jeopardization of labor' has also been accelerated by the abdication of the state from the sphere of labour regulation, through the privatisation of so-called activation measures and through the lens of suspicion with which it views youth. In terms of regulation, old legislative protections have been stripped away, while there has been a failure to legislate to protect workers exposed to new conditions, such as zero hours contracts. Of course, one could argue that it is in the short-term political interests of governments to ignore the increase in casualisation and the growth of part-time working: like those who remain in education, young people in precarious jobs are not claiming benefits and not inflating the politically sensitive unemployment figures.

Privatisation of training for young people who experience unemployment has led to the development of a highly profitable unemployment industry, which through recycling is able to profit through a failure to place young people in stable jobs. Government tolerance (and direct funding) of a scheme like the Work

Programme, with its 2 per cent 'success rate', shows how little the government is concerned about quality training for young people. Finally, an approach to young people who suffer the misfortune of becoming unemployed that regards them with suspicion, as 'wasters' to be battered into submission by a punitive and unsympathetic system, is at best counterproductive. It can force people to take up useless work experience programmes and reduce their ability to engage in effective job search activities.

In contemporary capitalist societies, even outside periods of recession, there are never enough jobs for all who want them, and many of those in jobs will find themselves with insufficient hours and with wages that are too low to maintain a decent standard of living. With a tradition of focusing on unemployment as one of the most visible manifestations of marginalisation, governments of all persuasions have helped sustain a discourse in which individuals are blamed for their predicament and treated with suspicion as work-shy parasites, thus justifying a punitive approach to benefit eligibility. These processes greatly impact on young people, as they are in transition and, therefore, more likely than older age groups to find themselves out of work or working in insecure forms of employment.

As Castel reminds us, the focus on unemployment and the use of terms such as marginalisation can be misleading 'for it displaces to the margins of society what is really something at its very heart' (2003: 367). In many parts of the global North, the jeopardised sector represents the new reality for young people. Within this sector, recurrent unemployment is commonplace, while employment lacks security. There is still room for some in the shrinking secure sector, although places are largely reserved for those whose parents are rich in cultural and economic capital. In the next chapter, we present some new analysis to highlight the condition of young people in the contemporary United Kingdom.

## Note

1   Low-paid industries are defined by the TUC as industries where average gross hourly pay falls below the 25th percentile (£7.95).

# Chapter 5

# The age of liminality

Binary oppositions ... are well suited to exaggerating differences, confounding description and prescription, and setting up overburdened dualisms that erase continuities, underplay contingency, and overestimate the internal coherence of social forms.

(Wacquant, 2008: 233–234)

## Introduction

In the post-recession United Kingdom, conditions that can be linked to the policies of austerity followed by the Coalition government up to 2015 and the Conservative government from May 2015 mean that many young people's lives are characterised by hardship and uncertainty. Yet, to an extent, uncertainty has always been central to the experience of being a young person: even in times of prosperity, outcomes and destinations were unpredictable for large sections of the young population. Young people inhabit a zone where their futures are represented as hopes or fears; and research conducted long before the recent recession has shown how even those from very privileged families worry about their futures (e.g. Walkerdine *et al*. 2001).

Of course, outcomes become even more uncertain in times of economic instability. In such times, young people have difficulty securing work may be forced to work in jobs that they regard as unsuited to their skills and qualifications or may prolong their educational careers as a way of sheltering themselves from the real or imagined turbulence of a tightening labour market. In such circumstances, young people may regard their current situation as temporary, while worrying about the unpredictability of future prospects.

Youth and young adulthood are temporary phases in the life course, and levels of employment continually rise and fall, making predictions difficult. When good times prevail, periods of uncertainty may be relatively brief, while in hard times they may be extended. Following the early 1980s recession there was a debate among youth sociologists, led by David Ashton and colleagues (1990) and David

Raffe (1986), which focused on the question of whether we were living through a period of temporary turmoil or whether we had crossed a watershed in which opportunities had been permanently transformed in ways that were unfavourable to both current and future generations.

On one side of the debate, Ashton and colleagues were arguing that the increase in youth unemployment was a consequence of long-term processes of change within capitalist economies; they saw high rates of unemployment as being a permanent feature of the new post-recession world order. They argued that

> we are currently witnessing a radical restructuring of the labour market in general and the youth labour market in particular. [Leading to] fundamental underlying structural changes which have produced a mismatch between the supply flow of young people entering the labour market and the demands of employers.
> (Ashton *et al.* 1990: 2)

Raffe (1986), on the other side, argued that the increase in unemployment was linked to the recession and was, therefore, a temporary phenomenon. In a sense, both arguments contained some truth: Raffe was right to argue that unemployment rates would fall significantly in the post-recession era, but Ashton and colleagues were correct to argue that there were far-reaching processes of change that would continue to impact on young people following the recession.

Through an analysis of the UK Household Longitudinal Study (known as Understanding Society) data, in this chapter we further explore patterns of insecurity in the contemporary UK labour market and its implications for the social condition of young people.

## Insecurity and flexibility

One of the questions that youth researchers are asking today again relates to the extent to which changes that we can observe now, notably the growth of temporary, part-time and atypical forms of employment, mark the contours of a future marked by lifetime uncertainty and hardship for large sections of the population. Guy Standing (2011) has been particularly vocal in his view of a future marked by growing precarity. In a similar vein, sociologists such as Ulrich Beck (2000) have argued that Western labour markets are moving closer to those represented by developing countries such as Brazil, where job insecurity is ubiquitous. These views are not without their merits: while accelerated by the recession, it is clear that the trend towards more precarious forms of working predated the recession (e.g. Furlong and Kelly 2005). Such conditions are not the preserve of a poorly skilled underclass; they have become common among young people from a wide range of social classes and from across the attainment spectrum. The benefits to business of a shift towards greater use of temporary and non-traditional employment contracts are clear:

> For businesses, this creates 'flexibility'. Fixed (or sticky) labour costs can be rendered variable; workplace discipline and control can be exercised individually (and indeed daily); some of the risks and costs associated with demand fluctuations can be externalised to the workforce; employment relationships can be initiated and terminated at will.
>
> (Theodore and Peck 2014: 26)

While some of the most influential names in sociology have argued that increased insecurity of labour has to be regarded as one of the core components of late modernity (e.g. Giddens 1990; Beck 1992; Sennett 1998; Bauman 2000), others have argued that theory is running ahead of empirical evidence. In an important contribution to the debate, Fevre (2007) is quite clear in his view that there is a lack of evidence to support the claim that employment insecurity has increased in either the United Kingdom or the United States. However, Fevre (2007) employs a narrow definition of insecurity, although he does explore both objective and subjective dimensions.[1] On the surface, his argument looks plausible; however, he defines insecurity in a way that leads to the exclusion of work situations that are important for young people, notably part-time jobs and training schemes, which tend to regarded as temporary even if the contractual situation is secure. Indeed, when Castel (2003) speaks of the 'jeopardization of labor', his focus is not just about temporary contracts but refers to atypical work which may be fixed-term, but may also be part-time or 'offered' under an activation programme. For young people, underemployment, in the sense of wanting more hours than are available or being employed in occupations that are way beneath what they would expect on the basis of their qualifications, may also be regarded as features of insecurity: while these folk may have permanent contracts, they probably regard their status as temporary, or at least hope that it is.

MacDonald (2016) describes a broad variety of approaches to insecurity employed by researchers that include a wide range of factors that go beyond impermanence and include a lack of social benefits, low wages, health risks, and being 'over-qualified' for a job. Reviewing young people's situations across Europe, MacDonald suggests that in the United Kingdom, 'the problem was less about the prevalence of temporary work and more of over-qualification for the sorts of jobs that were available' (2016: 158); in other words, the temporal insecurity that may be linked to the hope that a specific job is temporary and that more skilled employment will become available.

Further, defending Sennett against Fevre's accusations that his work lacks a firm empirical foundation, Tweedie argues that a narrow focus in insecure tenure misses the point: 'for Sennett, the harms flexible management practices cause workers stem from the destruction of routine work *time*' (2013: 97) and by under-mining people's ability to construct meaningful life narratives. In the literature on youth, the unsettling effects of the changes relate not so much to contractual issues but to the desychronisation of lives with family and friends (Woodman 2012) and the reduced control over lives in a broad sense; factors that can be credited to part-time work and subjective temporality as well as to contractual insecurity.

In the United Kingdom, much recent attention has been given to one particular form of atypical employment: zero hours contracts. With a zero hours contract, employers are not obliged to offer a fixed number of weekly hours to employees, even offering them no hours at all in a particular day, week or month if that suits the business. Such contracts are not necessarily temporary in nature. It has also become clear that some major employers rely very heavily on zero hours con-tracts: Sports Direct employs 23,000 workers, mainly young people, and 90 per cent of them are said to be on zero hours contracts that provide no guarantees of regular work. Many workers on zero hours contracts, as well as those on more traditional part-time contracts, would prefer to work full-time hours and can be considered to be underemployed.

Standing (2011) refers to the increasing population holding fixed-term, flex-ible and insecure employment contracts, as well as those with part-time jobs who desire full-time employment, as the precariat. With much of the growth in jobs in the post-recession UK occurring in low-skill and insecure sectors of the economy, his line of argument has its attractions. Yet, Standing regards the precariat as a 'class' or as having 'class characteristics' (2011: 8), even recognising, as he does, that they are 'far from being homogenous' (2011: 12); he paints a picture of a powerless group who 'lack a work-based identity' (2011: 12), powerless victims robbed of agency by an all-powerful capitalist class and the governments that serve its interests.

However, there are important sources of internal differentiation that are sus-tained by various forms of capital which lead us to question the idea that there has been a 'democratisation of insecurity' (Brown *et al.* 2003: 108) or whether the precariat can be regarded as a class. There are crucial differences between workless young people who lack skills and qualifications and graduates working in part-time or temporary forms of employment, as Max Weber would remind us: differences that relate to the ways in which education and skills are commodities of value to be traded on the labour market. To present the precariat as a class is to suggest that an unqualified young person working on a zero hours contract flipping burgers at McDonald's occupies a similar position to a pilot on a zero hours con-tract working for Ryanair. In a recent report to the European Commission, Jorens and colleagues (2015) argued that nearly one in two pilots working for low-fare European airlines were on temporary contracts, were self-employed or recruited through agencies. While job insecurity among pilots may be a cause for concern, as a group they may command relatively high wages and probably possess a strong work-based identity.

In our view Standing, disregarding Wacquant's (2008) warning about the dangers of binary oppositions, has tended to simplify a trend that is much more nuanced than he is prepared to recognise. Here, in exploring the conditions experienced by young people in the contemporary UK labour market, we look more closely at the stratification of the labour market for young people and of the factors that determine their distribution across sectors.

## Young people and segmented disadvantage

Starting from the position that all young people face uncertainties, with some clearly more vulnerable than others on account of the capitals they possess, in Chapter 3 we suggested that a series of risk zones can be identified, with placement in zones and movement between them conditioned by social, cultural and human capital and taking place within spatial horizons that give rise to different opportunity structures. The relative sizes of these zones differ over time and between places, but we would concur with Standing's position that there has been a trend towards the growth of zones characterised by insecurity and marginalisation. These zones, which we described with reference to the 1980s in Chapter 3, are represented using contemporary data in Figure 5.1.

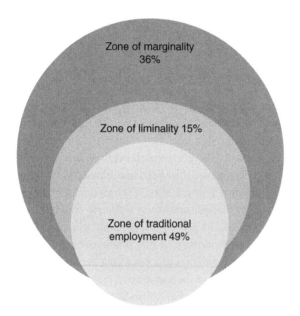

*Figure 5.1* Zones of (in)security (2010)

Using data from the first wave of Understanding Society (2010) for 18- to 25-year-olds, the relative size of each of the zones is shown in Figure 5.1. As in Chapter 3, we defined the zone of marginality as[2]

- the formally unemployed and those without any paid work;
- the sick and disabled;
- those on maternity leave or caring for others;
- those on government training or work experience schemes; and
- those working fewer than 16 hours a week.[3]

This group accounts for 36 per cent of the population of young adults, with the formally unemployed being the largest sub-group (52 per cent of the group). The zone of marginality is skewed towards females (56 per cent vs 44 per cent), largely on account of their over-representation in caring activities. One in four of this group (26 per cent) had never held any form of paid employment.

What we define as the zone of liminality represents 15 per cent of the 18- to 25-year-old population and members are defined as

- those whose contract of employment is time limited in any way (e.g. temporary contracts, agency hires etc.); and
- those working at least 16 hours per week but less than 30.

The zone of liminality is skewed slightly towards those on temporary contracts over those working part-time hours, and the group is skewed towards females (58 per cent vs 42 per cent).

As a group who are either unemployed, in receipt of benefits or working very few hours, the marginalised group are deprived economically. Nearly eight in ten (78 per cent) had a gross income of less than £670 per month, a sum that represents 60 per cent of the gross income of a worker in an elementary service occupation (defined here as poverty wages); a further one in five (19 per cent) received between £670 and £1200, which represents 60 per cent of the UK median wage in 2010 (referred to here as the economically challenged).

Those in the zone of liminality were better off financially, although six in ten (58 per cent) received poverty wages, and a further four in ten (38 per cent) were economically challenged. While marginalised females received slightly higher levels of income than males (a figure that will be skewed by child benefits), in the zone of liminality females were worse off economically than males.

In this model, Standing would regard these two outer zones (what we refer to as the zones of liminality and marginality) as representing the 'precariat'; we suggest that there are important lines of differentiation that justify the division that we make. Young people working very few hours, those without work or on government schemes tend to have less control over their lives than those whose conditions are insecure or who are underemployed and working between 16 and 30 hours a week. Indeed, those on benefits face punitive conditions: from 2011 they could be forced to work for 30 hours a week for 4 weeks under the threat of having their benefits stopped, a sanction that is brought to bear on those who miss or are late for appointments with their advisor or who are not deemed to be sufficiently engaged in job search activities.

An analysis by the *Guardian* newspaper suggests that in the year ending April 2014, one in six jobseekers were sanctioned by having their payments stopped (Butler and Malik 2015). These so-called mandated workers are expected to undertake work for the benefit of the community while continuing their job search in the reduced time available.

> I worked in admin since leaving college. It's all I've ever done and to be honest, it's what I'm good at, it's all I want to do. I lost my job at an estate agents in the recession and had to go on Jobseekers. I was asked what jobs I was looking for and I told them admin, secretarial and personal assistant work. What I'm qualified and experienced in. They sent me to work for a supermarket for four weeks. I had no choice or I'd lose my money. I finished it last week and was told there was no job at the end as I didn't have enough 'retail experience'. What was the fucking point of that?
>
> (Boycott Workfare)

Mandated workers are severely constrained in that they have no choice about the type of work they do: in one well-publicised case, a graduate, Cait Reilly, who had arranged her own work experience in a museum, was forced to work stacking shelves in Poundland under threat of benefit sanction. Workers who are mandated under UK workfare policies would appear to fall into the International Labour Office's definition of forced labour. Under the Forced Labour Convention (1930, No. 29), ratified by 177 states, forced labour is defined as 'all work or service that is extracted from any person under the menace of any penalty and for which the said person has not offered himself voluntarily'. A subsequent supplement to the convention (1957, No. 105) makes it clear that forced or compulsory labour is prohibited where it is used as a 'punishment for the infringement of labour discipline' (ILO 2014). Compared to mandated workers and others who occupy the zone of marginality, young people in the zone of liminality would appear to have greater control over their lives, with some accepting low-waged part-time or temporary work as a way of freeing themselves from reliance on a punitive welfare system.

## Beyond marginality and precarity

Beyond what Standing would refer to as the precariat (and what we refer to as the zones of liminality and marginality), roughly one in two 18- to 25-year-olds were in full-time permanent employment (referred to here as the traditional zone) (49 per cent), with males being much more likely than females to be working full-time on a permanent basis (57 per cent compared to 43 per cent). Those in the traditional zone were roughly divided between those receiving more than 60 per cent of the median wage (£1,200) and the economically challenged. Adding economically challenged full-time employees to those in the zones of liminality and marginality means that around three in four 18- to 25-year-olds have to cope with trying circumstances.

With educational qualifications being a strong determinant of young people's distribution across zones, it is clear that human capital offers some protection from liminality and marginalisation. Compared to those with higher level qualifications (A levels, degrees or equivalent), those with lower level qualifications (General Certificate of Secondary Education or lower) were around twice as likely to occupy the zone of marginality (52 per cent vs 25 per cent). While almost six in ten (58 per cent) young people with high-level qualifications were in full-time employment with permanent contracts, of those with lower level qualifications around a third (34 per cent) were similarly employed. In other words, there are still potential rewards to be gained through investment in education, even though gains are not guaranteed. In this context, it is important to be aware of a process of qualification inflation, whereby higher level qualifications become necessary to be considered for jobs that once required fairly minimal qualifications. Drawing on the UK Skills and Employment Surveys, which include workers of all ages, Gallie and colleagues argue that

> The qualification requirements of jobs in Britain have moved upwards since 1986. However, the trend became even more pronounced between 2006 and 2012. Jobs requiring no qualifications on entry fell from 28% in 2006 to 23% in 2012, while jobs requiring degrees or higher rose from a fifth (20%) in 2006 to a quarter (26%) in 2012. At no time in the 1986-2012 period have falls and rises of these magnitudes been recorded.
>
> (2014: 209)

Moreover, this process of qualification inflation has impacted on part-time employment: 63 per cent of part-time jobs required no specific qualifications in 1986, while by 2012 just 30 per cent could be secured without qualifications (Gallie *et al.* 2014).

Area of residence was also an important predictor of employment status (Figure 5.2). Both in labour markets characterised by low employment and those

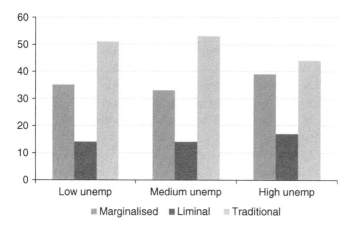

*Figure 5.2* Employment status by levels of unemployment in the local labour market

characterised by medium unemployment,[4] around one in two young people were in the traditional zone, compared to just over four in ten residents (44 per cent) of high unemployment areas. In high unemployment areas, more young people occupied the marginalised zone, while the size of the zone of liminality was also slightly larger in high unemployment areas. Residential capital is important, although weaker than educational capital, just as it was in the work conducted by Ashton and colleagues and Roberts in the 1980s, which we discussed in Chapter 3.

As young people are in a state of transition, over time we would expect to find movement from the zones of liminality and marginality towards more stable employment positions and see people successfully secure permanent jobs. A simple breakdown by age shows that younger age groups are more strongly clustered within the marginalised zone and the older age groups represented and more thinly represented in the traditional zone (Figure 5.3). For example, while just under one in two 18- and 19-year-olds were in marginalised positions (48 per cent), the corresponding figure for 24- and 25-year-olds was 28 per cent. While just over three (32 per cent) in ten 18- to 19-year-olds had full-time permanent jobs, nearly six in ten (58 per cent) 24- to 25-year-olds occupied such positions. However, with graduates entering the labour market from their early twenties onwards, movement from marginalised to core positions is likely to be exaggerated in this graph, as the populations in the two time periods are significantly different.

To assess levels of movement from the zones of liminality and marginality into the traditional zone, it is necessary to use a longitudinal perspective (Table 5.1). Taking those young people who were aged 20–21 at wave 1 and tracking them through to age 23–24 at wave 4, we find that more than half of those who occupied marginalised positions at wave 1 also occupied marginalised positions at wave 4

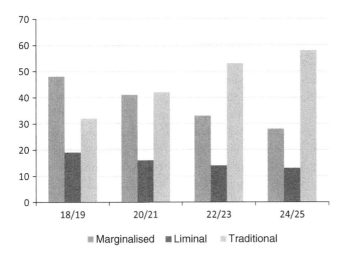

*Figure 5.3* Employment status by age

*Table 5.1* Employment status of individuals at wave 4 (aged 23–24) compared to wave 1 (20–21)

| | Wave 4 | | | |
| --- | --- | --- | --- | --- |
| *Wave 1* | *Marginalised* | *Liminal* | *Traditional* | *n* |
| All | | | | |
| Marginalised | 56 | 18 | 26 | 180 |
| Liminal | 18 | 37 | 44 | 54 |
| Traditional | 10 | 6 | 83 | 169 |
| Males | | | | |
| Marginalised | 45 | 11 | 45 | 80 |
| Liminal | 19 | 6 | 75 | 16 |
| Traditional | 7 | 6 | 87 | 101 |
| Females | | | | |
| Marginalised | 66 | 24 | 10 | 101 |
| Liminal | 18 | 50 | 32 | 38 |
| Traditional | 16 | 7 | 77 | 69 |

(56 per cent), one in four had moved into the traditional zone (26 per cent) while almost one in five (18 per cent) had moved into the liminal zone.

Among those in the zone of liminality at wave 1, over four in ten (44 per cent) had moved into the traditional zone, while nearly one in five (18 per cent) now occupied marginalised positions: nearly four in ten (37 per cent) remained in the liminal zone. A strong majority of those in the traditional zone at wave 1 were in the same position at wave 4 (83 per cent), although 6 per cent had moved into the zone of liminality and one in ten (10 per cent) were in marginalised positions. In other words, there is clear evidence of a scarring effect whereby early disadvantages seem to colour subsequent experiences.

There are quite striking differences here between males and females. Specifically, over the four years, 45 per cent of males as compared to 10 per cent of females moved from marginalised to traditional zones, with those females who did move out of the zone of marginality being much more likely than males to move from the marginalised to the liminal zone (24 per cent vs 11 per cent). Three in ten males (75 per cent) who occupied the liminal zone at wave 1 were in full-time permanent employment at wave 4, compared to a third (32 per cent) of females. Over the period males were more likely to remain in the traditional zone (87 per cent vs 77 per cent): a move partly reflecting the number of females who were withdrawing from the labour market to care for a family.

In sum, the figures clearly show that young people (especially females) who enter disadvantaged positions in the labour market find it difficult to move into full-time permanent jobs, while the vast majority of those who manage to enter secure positions at an early stage retain their advantaged positions.

## The social condition of young people in the contemporary labour market

Evidence from a wide range of countries and stretching back several decades demonstrates a clear link between job quality and psychological well-being and physical health (e.g. Banks and Ullah 1988), especially in relation to control over tasks and the ability to influence work-related decisions. Using well-validated scales developed by Warr (1990) on nationally representative data relating to all-age employees, Green and colleagues (2014) argued that between 2006 and 2012 there was a significant decline in job-related well-being. Using the same data, Gallie and colleagues (2014) show that over the same period there was an increase in job intensity (more people reporting that their job involved 'hard work'), a (smaller) rise in the numbers reporting that they worked under pressure due to tight deadlines and, for men, an increase in the number working in 'high strain jobs' (jobs that involved low levels of control as well as high work intensity). Over this period, there was no change in task discretion, although the authors note that with a rise in qualification requirements over the same period they would have expected to see an increase in task discretion. Finally, Gallie and colleagues note that people's fear of losing their jobs was higher in 2012 than in any other year covered by the surveys, 'including 1986 when unemployment rates were very much higher' (2014: 218).

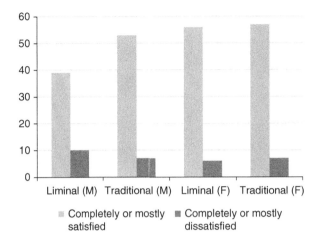

*Figure 5.4* Gender and employment status, by satisfaction with current job

Whereas we expected to find sharp differences in reported satisfaction with current jobs between those in the traditional zone and those in the zone of liminality, very similar numbers expressed dissatisfaction with their jobs: among the males, 10 per cent of those in the zone of liminality were dissatisfied compared to 7 per cent in the traditional zone; among the females the corresponding figures were 6 per cent and 7 per cent (Figure 5.4). However, the other end of the scale, males in the traditional zone were far more likely than those in the zone of liminality to report feeling mostly or completely satisfied (53 per cent vs 39 per cent), with the corresponding difference for females being almost non-existent (57 per cent vs 56 per cent).

Overall satisfaction with life was relatively high irrespective of employment status, with more than one in two males and females (50 per cent and 54 per cent, respectively) saying that they were completely or mostly satisfied with life. At the other extreme, just 4 per cent of males and 3 per cent of females reported that they felt completely or mostly dissatisfied with their lives. However, for males and females, those in traditional employment were most likely to express satisfaction and least likely to express dissatisfaction, while those in marginalised positions were least likely to report satisfaction and most likely to report dissatisfaction (Figure 5.5).

Overall, nearly one in two young people reported often or mostly feeling optimistic about the future (47 per cent of males and 52 per cent of females), although almost one in five said that they either rarely or never felt optimistic (17 per cent of males and 14 per cent of females). Feelings of optimism about the future were more positive among those in traditional employment, with little difference between males and females (Figure 5.6). While more than one in two traditional employees

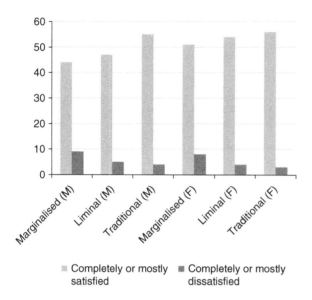

Figure 5.5 Gender and employment status, by whether completely satisfied with life

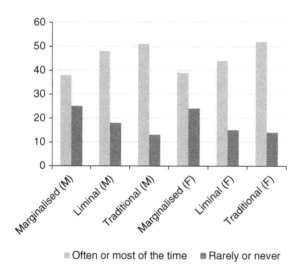

Figure 5.6 Gender and employment status, by optimism about the future

said that they often, or mostly, felt optimistic about the future, less than four in ten young people in marginalised positions felt this way. Conversely, around one in four young people in marginalised positions (25 per cent of males and 24 per cent of females) said that they never or rarely felt optimistic about the future, compared to 13 per cent of males and 14 per cent of females in traditional employment.

Levels of optimism among those in the zone of liminality were closer to those in the marginalised zone than they were to those in traditional employment.

While young people are often quite resilient, it is clear that employment status can impact on subjective well-being and mental health. Asked whether they had felt downhearted and depressed over the last 4 weeks, marginalised males and females were four times more likely than those in traditional employment to reply that they always or mostly felt this way (Figure 5.7). However, to put this into perspective, even among those marginalised, one in two males (51 per cent) and more than four in ten females (43 per cent) said that they never felt downhearted and depressed (the corresponding figure among those in full-time permanent employment being, respectively, 57 per cent and 48 per cent).

For young people, especially those who lack significant financial obligations, overall satisfaction with life and feelings of depression may be affected by factors other than job quality or employment security: leisure, time spent with friends and family and the ability to pursue non-work-related interests may be prioritised.

Overall, around a third of respondents said that they were mostly or completely satisfied with the amount of leisure they had, although those in traditional employment were less satisfied than the other two groups, suggesting that full-time employment had a detrimental effect on leisure time with some benefits in terms of leisure evident among those in the liminal and marginal zones (Table 5.2).

One of the consequences of exclusion from full-time employment relates to levels of income. Almost one in four young people in marginalised positions were completely or mostly dissatisfied with their incomes (23 per cent of males and

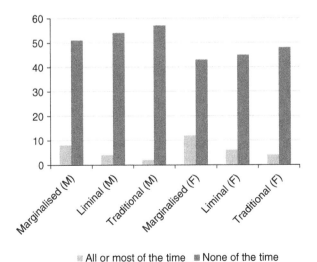

Figure 5.7 Gender and employment status, by feeling downhearted and depressed over the last 4 weeks

*Table 5.2* Gender and employment status, by satisfaction with amount of leisure time

|  | Males | | Females | |
| --- | --- | --- | --- | --- |
|  | Mostly or completely satisfied | Mostly or completely dissatisfied | Mostly or completely satisfied | Mostly or completely dissatisfied |
| Marginalised | 44 | 10 | 35 | 11 |
| Liminal | 44 | 10 | 35 | 11 |
| Traditional | 30 | 11 | 28 | 14 |

*Table 5.3* Gender and employment status, by satisfaction with income

|  | Males | | Females | |
| --- | --- | --- | --- | --- |
|  | Mostly or completely satisfied | Mostly or completely dissatisfied | Mostly or completely satisfied | Mostly or completely dissatisfied |
| Marginalised | 21 | 23 | 22 | 24 |
| Liminal | 31 | 12 | 22 | 12 |
| Traditional | 31 | 11 | 29 | 11 |

24 per cent of females), being around twice as likely to express dissatisfaction as compared to those in the liminal zone or in traditional employment (Table 5.3). The differences in levels of satisfaction expressed by traditional employees compared to those in the liminal zone were almost non-existent, suggesting that those in part-time and temporary forms of employment are relatively satisfied with their income (and of course, those with more than one part-time job may not suffer in terms of earnings).

## Boiled frogs: the new normality?

Some commentators recognise that the trend towards an increased insecurity of employment preceded the Great Recession, while arguing that an acceleration of the trend was attributable to the economic downturn: this is a view to which we subscribe. Influential social scientists, such as Standing and Beck, are also of the view that the tendency for precarious forms of employment to grow will continue and is probably irreversible: we also accept that this is a likelihood. However, we also suggest that these trends have such deep roots that young people have gradually built the changing realities into their expectations. In other words, young people have not suddenly found themselves having to cope with a radically altered set of realities (with all of the implications for subjective adjustments and well-being which may be triggered): the metaphor of the frog placed in a pan of cold water which is heated gradually until it is cooked to death *vis à vis* the frog dropped in boiling water that jumps out immediately is particularly apt.

With changes having taken place very gradually, we argue that on a subjective level, transitions are often accomplished without any major shocks, in a similar manner to that highlighted by Ashton and Field (1976). In other words, today, as in the 1960s, the realities encountered more or less confirm expectations. With parents of contemporary youth likely to have experienced high levels of unemployment themselves as school leavers, it is also likely that families help reinforce the view that transitions can be difficult to accomplish and security can be elusive.

Standing's (2011) views about the implications of contemporary labour market conditions imply that people have been taken by surprise by changing opportunity structures and are either projecting their frustrations outwardly as anger or internally in the form of subjective distress. Here, Standing refers to the four As that represent potential responses of the precariat to their suffering. These are

- anxiety, which stems from the economic uncertainty;
- anomie, as life comes to be seen as lacking meaning;
- alienation, as they lack control over their employment situations and work under conditions that are not of their choosing; and
- anger, as they realise that avenues to security are blocked and that the future is marked by relative deprivation.

It is true that, placed in situations where outcomes are unclear, young people can feel under pressure and may suffer from a decline in subjective well-being. As our earlier analysis showed, those occupying the most disadvantaged positions in the labour market tended to display the lowest satisfaction with life, tended to be least optimistic and had the poorest mental health, as measured on the General Health Questionnaire scale. At the same time, most young people were satisfied with their lives, and levels of optimism were high.

Our boiled frog hypothesis can be explained by Hall and colleagues' (2013) description of the ways in which sets of beliefs become embedded in our assumptive worlds and accepted as common sense. While Hall and colleagues (2013) are referring to the ways in which the core tenants of neo-liberalism, the market economy, free trade and the primacy of the private sector have become embedded in our beliefs, we suggest that there are sets of assumptions about the importance of Fordist employment models that may have been regarded as part of the natural order by those coming of age in the 1960s and 1970s which are no longer part of the assumptive worlds of young people today.

In this context, Wierenga warns that 'it is too easy to uncritically draw on paradigms that celebrate full-time work as a norm and as *the* measure of success' (2009: 118, original emphasis). Indeed, the young Australians that Wierenga studied were clear in their view that 'working is not the aim of life' (2009: 118); she stresses the importance of 'meaning, livelihood, connectedness, multi-dimensional lives and work-life balance' (2009: 118). In another Australian study, Stokes argued that employment instability, what Standing would term precarity, is not necessarily regarded by contemporary youth as unfavourable: 'many young people embrace flexibility as a way of life and view commitment to a single occupation for life as boring, or not allowing the possibility of achieving balance with the many commitments in a young person's life' (2012: 78).

It is true that processes of casualisation are far more advanced in Australia than in the United Kingdom (Furlong and Kelly 2005), and with employers being legally obliged to pay casual workers a 'penalty' wage loading, some young people may prefer to trade the entitlements that come with a full-time post (such as holiday pay and sick pay) for an hourly wage supplement in the order of 20 per cent.[5]

Although the Australian context is different, research in the United Kingdom has reached similar conclusions regarding young people's attitudes towards non-permanent employment. In a study of young people in Bristol, Bradley, for example, argued that even where young people held insecure or precarious jobs, they did not necessarily regard their situations negatively and were not 'distressed by their circumstances' (2005: 111), and many maintained a high degree of optimism about their futures.

The new normalities that underpin the assumptions of contemporary youth can be observed right across the zones of (in)security outlined earlier in this chapter. Among those we might describe as 'protected', young graduates who have been able to draw on their families' social and financial capital and have taken the advice of governments to invest in their future prosperity and security through advanced education often do not expect major pay-offs. In a study of UK graduates in their mid-twenties, Brooks and Everett found that that their respondents regarded their degrees as a 'basic minimum' (2009: 337) which were unlikely to open doors to rewarding careers. As one of their respondents commented on their degree, 'it's not so much a unique thing anymore – but without it you're kind of a bit stuffed' (2009: 337). For these young graduates, job insecurity following graduation was an expected part of their early careers, even in high-status fields such as law, and was not necessarily viewed negatively. One young woman, for example, argued that

> I did really enjoy temping and I think it showed me what I was good at, the fact that I could get on with a variety of people … that I was very confident and capable in certain areas. It showed me things I definitely didn't want to do'.
>
> (2009: 340)

Young people with relatively poor qualifications and those living in areas of high unemployment who may be vulnerable tend to have an awareness of their disadvantaged position and, while they may maintain relatively high aspirations (Kintrea *et al.* 2015), their expectations are more realistic. Employment is often seen instrumentally, as a means to a comfortable life, rather than as a source of fulfilment. In a study of moderately qualified working-class young men, Roberts and Evans (2013) argue that their aspirations are modest and often focused on the mundane. As one of their respondents explained,

> I'm not some flashy fuck, I'm not gonna sit here and say I wouldn't like a big house and that, and a Merc or something, but it's not likely to happen. What I want more than anything is to just be able to have my own place eventually, be able to go and see my mates after work sometimes, sometimes stay in on my own … And, um, end up living with a girl I guess.

Those who occupy the zone of liminality cannot be regarded as a homogenous group; while they may share aspects of their current work situation, this zone includes those from middle-class families who, rightly or wrongly, regard their situations as temporary, as well as those from working-class families who may experience regular periods of unemployment punctuated by occasional periods of casual work throughout their working lives. One in five young people in this zone have degrees, and some will be building up portfolios of experience as part of a strategy to enter professional careers; others may lack any control over their situations and may even occupy mandated positions. The zone of liminality is not a democratised (Brown *et al.* 2003) state of insecurity.

Those suffering most from contemporary conditions are the one in three that occupy the zone of marginality. While the boundary between the zones of liminality and marginality is a leaky one, with significant two-way traffic, clearly those who occupy marginalised positions tend to have least control over their lives. Young people in this zone have long been the focus of policy, and there have been numerous (largely ineffective) attempts to move them into work through training programmes, to create intermediate labour markets to provide experience and to mandate unpaid work. Policy debates about this group tend to focus on individual deficits, be they skills, qualifications or attitudes. However, the academic literature clearly shows that the problem is on the demand side of the labour market rather than the supply side. While some young people in this zone lack qualifications, many are well qualified (one in ten are graduates).

In a study of two severely deprived areas of Glasgow and Teesside (Shildrick *et al.* 2012), young people who were long-term unemployed displayed a desperation to work, even when they were extremely pessimistic about their chances of finding a job. As one young man put it,

> if I could get a job I would stick to it and do anything I can just to keep it. I would like warehousing, like labourer, even sales assistant, just any job, cleaner. … You need a job just to grow up, more or less. If I got a job that would prove that could stand on my own two feet and things. A job isn't just a job, it's more than a job. It's the future of your life.

Unlike the other two zones in our model, the zone of marginality has not become normalised, nor is it democratised. Those without qualifications, from poor families and living in areas which have weak labour markets are over-represented, and, while worklessness is not uncommon, those affected rarely lose all hope to the extent that they regard it as a normal and accepted long-term status (Shildrick *et al.* 2012); and the association between unemployment and a declining sense of well-being are well-documented (e.g. Warr 1990).

Looking across the zones that make up this new landscape of (in)security, there is now a widespread belief that the ability to manage life projects through the development of effective navigation skills places an increased emphasis on the importance of agency in determining outcomes. The new language of policy incorporates these beliefs through the idea of employability. Employability is presented as an ability to gain and maintain employment; the skill to navigate opportunities and sell oneself as a desirable product. However, the idea reinforces the notion that a lack of employment or a turbulent career is the product of supply side deficits and overlooks the fact that

> employability will vary according to economic conditions. At times of labour shortages the long-term unemployed become 'employable'; when jobs are in short supply they become 'unemployable' because there is a ready supply of better qualified job seekers willing to take low-skilled, low-waged jobs'.
>
> (Brown *et al.* 2003: 110)

## Conclusion

In a context where flexibilisation and insecurity have become key features of the neo-liberal landscape, and hardship and insecurity are common among young people, we must be cautious about approaches that suggest there are moves towards a democratisation of insecurity involving a growing and relatively undifferentiated 'precariat'. Marginalisation, insecurity and risk are structured states, and human, social and cultural capital ultimately provide some protection for privileged groups. We see no merit in presenting as homogenous something that is essentially heterogeneous, indeed, it is a disservice to the truly disadvantaged (Wilson 1990) to suggest that their misfortunes are shared by a broader group who benefit from a range of resources that others are denied.

While employment conditions and prospects have deteriorated, and may well continue to deteriorate, many young people maintain their optimism and report satisfaction with their lives. While we argued that the gradual nature of the changes can be seen as confirmation of a boiled frog hypothesis, du Bois Reymond and Plug explain reactions as being part of a shift 'away from a work ethic to what we might term a combination ethic, stressing a balance of values and priorities' (2005: 56). Although many young people are able to ride above the turbulence of the labour market, we have argued that suffering is not uncommon, but nor is it universal. In other words, the changes we have described have consequences which extend beyond the material to the ways we engage subjectively with the world. For some young people, the importance of employment and work-based identities will be downgraded as they seek to find alternative sources of fulfilment; others will be consumed by anxieties and will suffer psychologically as they link their circumstances to their own actions rather than to external forces that are beyond their control.

## Notes

1  Defined by temporary contractual status, an understanding that a job was not permanent in some way, feelings of job insecurity or expectations of becoming unemployed in the next 12 months.
2  There are some small differences in the ways the zones were specified in the historical and contemporary data due to the ways that different variables were defined (e.g. part-time work can only be defined as less than or more than 10 in the historical data).
3  There is, inevitably, a degree of arbitrariness in deciding on an hours-based division, although those working fewer than 16 hours are unlikely to be able to sustain an above-poverty level of existence without a benefit or tax credit subsidy (and those working less than 16 hours are currently ineligible for benefits in the form of Working Tax Credits).
4  Official unemployment statistics pertaining to 2011 were assigned at the level of travel-to-work areas which were then aggregated to equal thirds to represent areas characterised by high, medium and low unemployment.
5  For example, an 18-year-old working as a retail store assistant would be entitled to a legal minimum wage of $12.97 per hour of he or she was employed on a full-time basis but $16.21 per hour on a casual contract.

# Chapter 6

# Towards a post-liminal labour market

> [H]owever utopian or unpalatable, costly or unrealistic, it might appear to us today, one thing is certain: as persistent and acute marginality of the kind that has plagued American and European cities over the past two decades continues to mount, strategies … will have to be reorganized in ways so drastic that they can hardly be foretold today.
>
> (Wacquant 2008: 255–256)

## Introduction

One of the key achievements of this book is to take a longer-term view of young people's experiences in a changing labour market in ways that are theoretically informed and empirically evidenced using legacy and contemporary data. In much of the literature, there has been a tendency to exaggerate trends and to make claims about the contours of a future labour market that are little more than speculative. Here, we have been able to take the long view, focusing on major recessions and periods of relative prosperity in a way that has allowed us to avoid being caught up in specific moments when the worlds that young people inhabit seemed to be changing in radical, even unpredictable, ways. Writing at a time when much of the world is still suffering from a global financial crisis and the implementation of severe austerity measures that often take the greatest toll on young people, we have been able to show that trends that accelerated from 2007–8 began several decades earlier; thus linking past, present and potential futures.

Our analysis demonstrated that the labour conditions faced by young people have deteriorated over the long term, that jobs have become less secure and that new forms of employment disempower and disenfranchise the young generation. Opportunities for young people frequently involve temporary contracts, part-time working and work in occupations that provide little in the way of intrinsic fulfilment. Despite huge investments in education, underemployment is common, and social mobility has stalled. Life management has become more complex, with changes in employment having implications for the establishment of relationships and independent living. These changes are not confined to a period of 'transition' during youth and young adulthood but fundamentally alter the life course.

The words used and the concepts developed to describe and capture the essence of new and emerging social realities have sometimes encouraged us to depart from empirical realities. Here we have taken issue with Guy Standing (2011) and the term he coined, 'the precariat'. While building on ideas with origins in French sociology that, rightly, alerted us to the ways in which 'new' conditions of labour simulated marginality and disempowered the working classes, Standing's mistake lay not in the way he moved forwards the debate about the jeopardisation of labour (Castel 2003) but in the implication that marginality was becoming democratised through merging the 'truly disadvantaged' (Wilson 1990) with those in insecure or 'atypical' forms of employment.

The marginalisation and suffering of those without work, those unable to work and those barely able to obtain sufficient hours of employment to obtain a decent standard of living, to adequately feed their families and to escape the punitive intrusions and frequent threats that emanate from the agents of welfare policy, are far from new: novelists such as Zola and Dickens and social scientists such as Marx and Engels and Seebohm Rowntree described conditions similar to those we observe today from the early days of the industrial revolution through to Europe in the post-Second World War era.

The working poor have always been with us, as has labour precarity. From seasonal agricultural work that long predated the industrial revolution to the casualised labour that was the norm in UK ports until Attlee's post-war Labour government introduced the National Dock Labour Scheme[1] as a means of guaranteeing dockers the legal right to minimum work, holidays and sick pay, 'precarious' work has always been part of the employment landscape.

While we accept that insecure, fragmented and non-standard forms of employment have been growing and accelerated in the aftermath of the Global Financial Crisis (GFC), we have argued that these trends have deep roots and that referring to this heterogeneous group of workers as 'the precariat' is misleading. The group of workers that stand between 'traditional' full-time employees and those who are workless, severely constrained or marginalised are an extremely varied group; certainly, some are little different from those who are marginalised and may experience regular churn between the two positions. Others, often those with human or cultural capital, pass through this zone fleetingly, or may represent a labour aristocracy of high-skill, high-wage workers in contract-based occupations such as broadcasting or pilots with budget airlines. Some young people who occupy this zone have made positive choices and may be taking control of a life that would otherwise be severely constrained through the practices of the agents of welfare policy. Not all young people want to live a life within the predictable parameters of a Fordist career where 1 day, 1 week, 1 month resembles the next. Indeed, some young people choose frugal lives and downgrade from 'traditional' jobs to McJobs in order to free 'temporal and mental space to be creative' and build lives that are fulfilling and hopeful outside of a normative employment nexus (Threadgold 2015).

Rather than use or adapt the term precarity that brings in its train uniformly negative connotations and suggests commonality of experience and even coherence as a collectivity, as argued in Chapter 3, we introduced the term liminality and the zone of liminality. In this way, we build on a solid anthropological tradition initiated by van Gennep (1960) in which he recognised the ways in which previous continuities and certainties are opened to challenge with fluid and malleable realities, or liquid modernity, to put it another way (Bauman 2000), representing new contexts in which lives are lived (with both positive and negative connotations).

Thus, the zone of liminality is a zone where outcomes are uncertain and in which people may develop a range of objective pathways which may be subjectively negotiated in a variety of ways. It is a zone which represents a changed reality, but also one that involves frequent changes in the ways in which individuals manage and interpret the foundations of their lives with the offer of a perspective free of the traditions of a Fordist life, which can be both liberating and threatening. For Turner (1969), the liminal stage can also lead to the emergence of new structures and changing hierarchies as people from different communities, or classes, are brought into new proximities. In the liminal zone, for example, young people from middle-class families with university degrees may find themselves working alongside early school leavers from poor families; even where these proximities are fleeting, they may bring about fresh understandings of populations that traditionally only mixed in hierarchical situations.

## Reflecting on change

One of the most significant changes affecting young people's experiences in the labour market, and their lives more generally, is the expansion of education. While it is true that recent increases in educational participation and attainment have not increased the prospects of social mobility, education can open horizons and impact on aspirations and expectations in work and non-work contexts. For those who go to university, if nothing else, the experience provides them with an expanded period between dependence and the burdens of domestic responsibility where they can contemplate future lives and dip their toes into the labour market. Yet, participation in higher education carries costs: most obviously, the implications of fee changes that mean many graduates emerge from university with significant debt that may restrict their ability to enter the housing market or may necessitate taking the first available job in order to service credit-card debts

(Furlong and Cartmel 2009). There are also potential subjective costs involved, where young people invest in an expected graduate career and find themselves working in routine, often insecure, forms of employment. However, there is some evidence that expectations have been depressed, with some seeing a degree as a minimum qualification rather than a clear route to a graduate career.

Both graduates and non-graduates frequently experience insecure and atypical forms of employment: for some, these are temporary and represent stepping stones to more traditional careers, whereas others are churned between insecure jobs and worklessness or remain in this liminal state in the long term. As employment opportunities have changed, so have subjective orientations. There is evidence that some young people regard the new landscape of employment as normal, and there are minority groups who use the changes to their advantage. At the same time, there is a clear downside reflected not just in financial health and security, but in subjective adjustments necessary to manage complex lives.

The ways in which governments have responded to various crises of employment and to the needs of vulnerable individuals have always been less than adequate. Policy has been framed under the assumption that improved situations can only be brought about by tackling an assumed deficit in the human capital possessed by young people rather than by addressing significant problems of demand. In policy, young people are regarded with suspicion, seen as work-shy and as not knowing what is best for themselves in the long term. Where training is provided, it is often of poor quality, delivered at a level that will not deliver any significant boost to human capital and 'offered' without due regard for the aspirations of the individual. Moreover, policies are often unsuited to modern-day circumstances in that they are underpinned by the idea that the labour market can be represented as a dichotomy between the employed and unemployed – or not in education, employment or training (NEET)/non-NEET – with the aim being to move people from a state of worklessness to employment. In policy, it is rare to see acknowledgement of a zone of liminality populated by a heterogeneous population with diverse needs, and there has been little serious effort to reframe policy in ways that acknowledge changed realities and new needs.

A strength of this volume is that it has enabled us to draw on previously underexploited data in order to provide an overview of young people's experiences of employment and unemployment and security and insecurity over time while highlighting macro-level changes and continuities. Data from two 1980s studies alongside that derived from a large-scale, nationally representative, contemporary dataset have given us an unprecedented understanding of the changing state of young people in the labour market.

Using data from the two periods, we introduced three zones of (in)security, facilitating a broad comparison of changes between two time periods (Table 6.1). This model takes us beyond the dualisms that have so far blinded us to the significance

*Table 6.1* Defining zones of (in)security: 1980s, 2010s

|  | *1980s* | *2010s* |
|---|---|---|
| Zone of traditionality | Full-time jobs with open-ended contracts. | Full-time jobs with open-ended contracts. |
| Zone of liminality | Employed on temporary contracts, working between 10 and 30 hours a week. | Employed on temporary contracts, working between 16 and 30 hours a week. |
| Zone of marginality | Unemployed (including those not formally registered as unemployed), the workless, on government schemes, working in 'fill-in jobs'. | Unemployed (including those not formally registered as unemployed), the workless (including sick and disabled and carers), on government schemes, working fewer than 16 hours a week. |

of the liminal zone and where young people survive in a space between security and insecurity and fall between the cracks in policy. Despite our best efforts, the accuracy of our comparisons is limited by the ways in which researchers, operating within the normative assumptions of the day, tried to capture the state of the labour market. Differences in the ways that information was captured reveal a change in some of the criteria used to define labour market positions, partly due to a tightening up of definitions used in the respective survey instruments, which themselves reflect policy changes over time, but also reflect one of the inevitable consequences of using datasets which were not designed for comparability and which reflect assumptions that were prevalent in the different periods. So, for example, the definition of part-time work changes over the period, and the criteria used to define the marginalised, particularly the definition of 'unemployment' and 'out of the labour force', became more nuanced as dualistic approaches started to be challenged.

Comparing the zones across time reveals a slight increase in the size of the zone of traditionality (45 per cent to 49 per cent), counterbalanced by a corresponding decrease in the number of young people in the marginalised zone where we find the workless and those working very few hours (43 per cent compared to 36 per cent) (Figure 6.1). Compared to the 1980s, the liminal zone has increased in size (from 12 per cent to 15 per cent). Clearly, changes are relatively small, and, in these two periods characterised by high youth unemployment, the similarities appear greater than the differences. However, the composition of the liminal zone does vary over time in that in the 1980s it was skewed towards part-time workers, whereas in the contemporary period it is skewed temporary work and casual workers. In both periods, it is women and those residing in the weakest labour markets that suffer most.

A particularly worrying change over time was the idea, introduced in Chapter 3, of a 'punitive turn' in policy triggered by a shift in policy and the underlying attitude from a culture of compassion to a culture of blame. The emergence of the new regime, palpable from the early 1980s, saw unemployed young people beginning

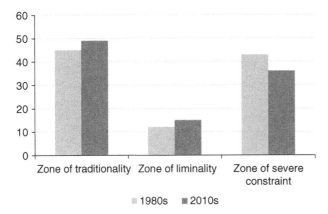

*Figure 6.1* Zones of (in)security: 1980s, 2010s

to be sanctioned for their failure to secure employment, for example, with the threat of benefits being withdrawn and work placements and training schemes becoming compulsory. This approach became more pronounced over time, as successive UK governments felt the need to control young people ever more closely. By 2011, sanctions included not simply the threat of cuts to benefit payments as suggested in the 1980s but the introduction of a range of forced labour schemes (e.g. the Help to Work Scheme) and full, long-term, withdrawal of state support as a sanction for non-compliance.

The treatment of young people in policy is directly linked to the neo-liberal agenda and the shift from collectivist to individualist perspectives. Citizens who push back against this agenda are faced with harsh sanctions and by ham-fisted attempts to force them to work within a policy agenda which many young people recognise as being irrelevant to the worlds they inhabit: effectively, civilising offences committed by the state against young people.

Despite an increase in educational participation over time, there has been relatively little reduction in the size and composition of the most disadvantaged group. In both periods, those young people who entered either of the insecure zones on leaving education had difficulties improving their position over time. The experience of being trapped in the marginalised zone or the liminal zone is further compounded for those living in depressed and declining labour markets where opportunities to move into the zone of traditionality are often scarce. By contrast, in both time periods, the young people who entered the zone of traditionality on leaving education were more likely to experience some stability, emphasising the importance of linear transitions from education to work rather than the non-linear alternatives involving greater insecurity (Furlong *et al.* 2003).

## Well-being

Alongside the increasingly hostile and punitive policy environment and a challenging labour market, recognition of the impact of labour market experiences on young people's psychological well-being received attention in both periods. In the 1980s, studies found that many young people were experiencing psychological difficulties adjusting to a new type of labour market (e.g. Banks and Ullah 1988), and this remained an issue for the 2010 generation (e.g. West 2009).

Currently, there is considerable concern about the mental health of young people, with special funding schemes for research launched recently in a number of countries, including the United Kingdom. This is unsurprising, as there is a wealth of evidence suggesting alarming levels of mental health issues among young people (West 2009; Eckersley 2009). Figures from Scotland, for example (which are not out of line with other countries in the global North), show that just over four in ten females and around a third of males show clinically significant levels of depression and anxiety (West 2009). There is a wide range of explanations for poor levels of well-being among young people, some of which relate to the labour market trends we have highlighted in this book.

Of particular significance are the ontological insecurities that arise as young people negotiate uncertain terrains in contexts where blame for failure rests on individuals, even when they have followed the best available advice and invested heavily in their own futures (Furlong and Cartmel 2007). Eckersley (2009) argues that personal control represents a significant protective factor for mental health and well-being, and where individuals have to negotiate fragmented experiences in the labour market and manage different components of their lives, then there are likely to be subjective consequences. In addition, Eckersley places some of the blame on a materialist culture, arguing that 'materialism (the pursuit of money and possessions) breeds not happiness, but dissatisfaction, depression, anxiety, anger, isolation and alienation' (2009: 357).

At the same time, the recent data that we analysed tended to suggest that many young people had adjusted to contemporary conditions – satisfaction with life and optimism regarding the future were not suggestive of an epidemic of misery. Despite reasonably healthy levels of satisfaction and optimism, a significant minority are badly affected by trends, especially those who occupy marginalised positions. Indeed, feelings of depression among the marginalised are four times higher than among those in full-time permanent employment.

There is a risk that the growing disjuncture between predominant policy discourses and the new normality is damaging to mental health as they can promote a sense that individual lives are unusual or flawed, even where they are clearly aligned with others members of their generation. There is still an assumption in policy that there is a gold standard of full-time, relatively stable employment that is attainable by all who make the necessary efforts and investments and display appropriate attitudes. Where the new normality is presented as inferior, obstacles are placed in the ways of individuals who are attempting to make fulfilling lives in circumstances that are not of their own choosing.

While it is entirely appropriate to draw attention to the ways in which labour market experiences can have damaging consequences for mental health, it is also important to recognise that, in both periods, levels of optimism were relatively high, and there was a sense that, for those entering the labour market in the 2010s, the challenging labour market conditions were simply 'normality' and something their own parents (many of whom were 1980s school leavers themselves) had been among the first to face.

## The future

If we accept the argument outlined in this book – that the current difficulties faced by young people in the labour market are not part of a fleeting turmoil being experienced in the wake of the GFC but are clear trends that can be traced back to the 1970s and 1980s, suggestive of a future trajectory that will see insecure and fragmented forms of employment continue to grow – then we need to consider the implications for the lives of both the young and the not-so-young in future decades. In the 'gig economy', people have to build their lives in new ways, both objectively, as they seek to establish an acceptably sound financial base to keep a roof over their heads and food in their mouths, and subjectively, as they create the sense of normality and personal control that underpins well-being.

A shift away from material culture is a possible response, and already there is evidence that some young people are choosing this path (Threadgold 2015). Of course, a mass move in this direction undermines a capitalist economy driven by the consumption of 'unnecessary' goods and services. Although yet to be fully implemented in a major economy, the idea of providing all citizens with a living allowance that they would supplement with employment (the unconditional basic income or citizens wage) in the gig economy or in more traditional spheres can be seen in this context as an aid to the survival of consumer capitalism.

While such a change in policy may appear unnecessarily radical and unaffordable, we have to remember that through taxation and welfare systems, in the United Kingdom the taxpayer already subsidises employers who operate low-wage regimes and helps keep families afloat when wages received are insufficient to provide a decent standard of living. We suggest that the time has come for a welfare revolution and for a rethink of the ways we regulate employment in the modern world. Properly constructed, this would not simply be about mitigating risk, but would be designed in such a way that new forms of creativity are unleashed and new freedoms established.

One of the messages that comes through from the research is that a move from policies underpinned by punitive measures has to be replaced by a more permissive approach so as to stimulate creative approaches to life management in an era characterised by increasingly diverse pathways. While doubts have long been expressed about the effectiveness of punitive approaches, such as workfare, they are framed within a set of Fordist assumptions under which life patterns displayed a greater uniformity: in the new normality, 'one size fits all' approaches are counterproductive.

Approaches to policy that are fit for purpose in the contemporary era are best framed in a 'bottom-up' fashion. In other words, they need to be flexible enough to help young people on their own terms; to assist their efforts to create the life that they wish to establish for themselves, be it one that is strongly work-centred or one that has a stronger focus on relationships or leisure.

While young people are quite resilient and show signs of having taken on board new realities, the pressures that can be harmful psychologically are often ones imposed by older people framing policy, providing education or within their own families. Carrying with them assumptive worlds framed in a disappearing era, in their dealings with young people they attempt to smooth entry into a world with which they are familiar, often with little understanding of the new formalities or the ways in which young people have accommodated these changes subjectively. Thus, improving well-being among young people can be brought about through policy change rather than through individualised interventions.

To an extent, the problems we see in policy are also manifest in some of the academic literature on young people in which fragmented and insecure work forms are seen as part of modern transitions rather than as a state of liminality that, for some, will last a lifetime. New research questions need to focus on the ways in which lives are built and sustained against a backdrop of ongoing liminality involving objective insecurity and subjective uncertainty.

In this book, we have been critical of Standing's (2011) portrayal of the precariat as a class and the underlying assumptions about the democratisation of disadvantage. For Standing, the precariat respond to their situation through anxiety, alienation, anomie and anger (reactions he refers to as the four As). Clearly, there are elements of all four responses among young people in the zones of marginality and liminality (as well as among some in secure employment); however, these states are far from universal, and even among the most disadvantaged groups we find evidence of positive adjustment and optimism. While Standing argues that anxiety, alienation, anomie and anger will increase as Fordist structures wither, he tends to overlook the resilience of youth and the creativity they employ to make lives in circumstances that older generations certainly regard as prejudicial to the establishment of a 'good' life.

While we are reluctant to end on a pessimistic note, recent indications suggest that the landscape of political discourse around opportunities for young people has changed little since the punitive turn, and the neo-liberal agenda is still being played out. In the United Kingdom, as in many other countries, the current policy framework is not fit for purpose, and much legislation is based on outdated assumptions. New protections for workers are long overdue, and punitive approaches are ineffective and 'drastic' measures are called for (Wacquant 2008: 56).

While educational participation has increased throughout this period, education is not only about employability and selectivity, or individualised social mobility, as such interventions will only reinforce the liminal characteristics of employment and young adulthood for many while alleviating it for increasingly few. Such education interventions are pointless without labour market interventions. As it stands, education simply extends the zone of liminality for the majority, with young people being 'neither one thing nor another' – neither students, workers nor unemployed, but at the same time all of these things.

Current labour market trends are not encouraging and make us mindful of Beck's vision of 'Brazilianization' in which large populations survive in poverty and live their lives under conditions of extreme unpredictability. A more positive way forwards has to begin to identity ways in which liminal lives can be sustainable and fulfilling lives.

## Note

1   The National Dock Labour Scheme was introduced in 1947 and, aside from guaranteeing minimum conditions, it also gave trade unions influence over recruitment and dismissal. It was abolished in 1989 by the Thatcher government, leading to widespread strike action.

# Is it inevitable that young people have to carry these costs of social change?

## Introduction

Over the past half-century, the United Kingdom has witnessed radical change in a number of areas, not least in the ways in which the production of goods and services has been organised. As with all social change, some groups carry the cost more than others. In this case, young people have been among the hardest hit. Yet, the ways in which politicians and ruling elites in the United Kingdom have tackled the ensuing problems have not changed significantly. Fifty years ago, young people's attitudes and behaviours were seen to be the cause of the problem. In the second decade of the twentieth century, this is still the case. Yet, this need not be so. In other societies, young people do not experience the same problems and anxieties that confront British youth.

## Globalisation

All industrial societies have faced the same changes over the last five decades resulting from the globalisation of production. Following the Second World War, production was organised on a nation-centric basis. Goods such as automobiles and white goods had their components produced and assembled in the country in which they were sold. The United Kingdom had its own producers, while foreign producers based in the United Kingdom, such as Ford, also produced the components and assembled them in the United Kingdom. Similarly, services such as banking and retail were organised around national markets (Ashton 2017, forthcoming). These large organisations provided the basis of relatively stable communities in which young people tended to follow their parents into permanent full-time jobs.

Over the last five to six decades, a whole series of changes under the label of globalisation have transformed these relationships. First, during the late 1960s and 1970s, the capital and the whole of the production of low-value goods such as textiles, shoes and bicycles were relocated to the 'developing' countries in

Asia, where labour costs were lower. As the authors illustrate in Chapter 2, for young people this spelt the end of thousands of permanent full-time jobs in routine semi-skilled and skilled production work. In the late 1980s and 1990s, the advent of the Internet and other developments in electronic technology created even more radical changes in the organisation of production. The control that employers were able to exercise over the production process through the use of this new information and computer technology enabled them to break down the process of production and locate the various components in different parts of the world, where the production costs per component item were lower; production was modularised (Berger 2006). This meant that some parts of the process remained in the older industrial countries (initially those requiring a high level of intellectual input), but other parts could be located elsewhere. Moreover, because employers had also learnt how to speed up the process of learning work-based skills, they could rapidly relocate the various parts of the process to other countries. These changes were facilitated by the progressive reduction of trade barriers between nations through the actions of transnational companies and organisations such as the World Trade Organisation. Trade between nations expanded rapidly – for example, between 1990 and 2010 global trade grew roughly twice as a fast as global GDP (Manyika *et al.* 2012: 73), a process that illustrated the growing interdependence of nations in the global economy. As this process affected more and more of the national economy, employment for both young people and adults became more insecure. By the twenty-first century, much of manufacturing and large areas of service production were organised on a global basis.

In the older industrial countries, these changes were also associated with a shift in the balance of power between the classes. Work by the Organisation for Economic Cooperation and Development (OECD) (2012) has shown that the proportion of national income going to labour has been falling since the 1990s in most OECD countries. In the early 1990s, labour received an average of 66 per cent of the national income, but by the early 2000s this had fallen to 62 per cent. Within the United Kingdom, as in some other societies, this fall in the share of labour in the national income is not uniform across all workers. The income of top earners has increased dramatically during this period (Atkinson *et al.* 2011), while the position of those at the bottom end of the distribution has been worsening (Atkinson 2015). For youths who are disproportionately found in low-wage occupations, the situation is even worse.

Other changes were also taking place in the organisation of production, namely the application of mass production techniques to the growing service sector and the increasing use of computer and Internet technologies to rationalise and routinise work in the retail, restaurant, hotel, travel and financial sectors. At the same time as economic growth and the application of digital technologies were increasing the proportion of knowledge-intensive jobs in the areas of management and technical and professional work, the new technologies were routinising many jobs in these areas and reducing skill levels as routine transactions were performed through the use of algorithms (Brown *et al.* 2011). Meanwhile, in the retail and restaurant trade, the use of mass production techniques together with the growth of personal service and care sectors were increasing the number of low-skilled jobs.

## National level

National governments responded differently to these pressures for change. How they responded depended on a number of factors, such as the values of the political elite and the existing institutional provision for education, welfare and workplace training. In the United Kingdom, the combination of the commitment to neo-liberal policies and the deregulation of the market for capital and labour led to the spread of flexible labour policies throughout the labour market and subsequent insecurity in employment. In this context, the responsibility for securing employment was transferred from the state to the individual. Young people were portrayed as solely responsible for investing in their education and training and securing their jobs. Consequently, any failure to achieve qualifications or a job was seen to result from personal deficiencies. This was not the case in other societies.

In Germany and Denmark, the political elites continued to support collaboration between the state, employers and unions in the implementation of employment policy and, to a lesser extent, welfare policy. These policies did not eradicate the trend towards greater flexibility in the use of labour or the widening of the gap between the classes, but as we shall see, they did contain it in different ways. For young people in these countries, it meant that while they came to be seen as partly responsible for investing in their education and training, the state continued to accept responsibility for ensuring that the worst effects of insecurity were mitigated during their transition into work.

## United Kingdom

In the United Kingdom, the powers of global capital to limit the powers of the state with regard to the movement of capital were extended by the political actions of the Conservative government through the privatisation of the public service industries and by the deregulation of the financial services. This led to a reduction of the influence of national values and pressures on companies which, 'freed' from these constraints, responded more to the financial pressures from global markets (Gomez and Korine 2008). There were a number of consequences of this enhanced leverage. One was that it contributed towards a more radical shift in the balance of power between employers and employees in the labour market than was observed in many other countries. As a result, the salaries of senior managers increased rapidly relative to that of their employees (Atkinson *et al.* 2011). The other was that many public companies, and the jobs they created in the labour market, became increasingly subject to short-term fluctuations in the financial markets. The jobs therefore offered less security for employees, not just the operatives but also middle managers and professional workers, generating more insecurity throughout the labour market (Clark and Heath 2014). At the same time, the powers of the unions were severely limited through legislation that reduced their ability to resist the accompanying changes in terms of conditions of employment. This also hindered their attempts to protect wages against the downward pressures created by companies using labour arbitrage to lower wage costs and through the use of immigrant labour that was used to create downward pressure on the wages of the lower skilled.

As Chapter 5 illustrates, young people were not passive recipients of these changes; many responded to these new pressures by extending their education. Encouraged by the raising of the school leaving age and persuasion from the government and media to invest in their own human capital, an ever-increasing proportion of them stayed on at school and later sought entry to higher education. As measured by educational achievement, the skill levels of the youth labour force were constantly increasing (Green 2006), although there remained a stubborn group of low achievers, while educational levels as measured by international comparisons remained low. For those who entered jobs at the top of the labour market, with private education and Oxbridge or Russell Group university degrees, the prospects were good and their income steadily increased. For those who entered in the middle and at the bottom of the labour market, the focus of this book, the situation was different. During the recessions of the late 1970s and the Great Recession of 2008, less than half the young people entered permanent, secure, full-time work. For the majority, the experience was one of unemployment, government schemes and temporary and part-time work. Moreover, these figures were an average; in some of the more depressed areas of the country in the 1980s, entry into full-time permanent work was available to only just over one in five. In the face of these new conditions of insecurity and casualised jobs, many remained satisfied with their lives and levels of optimism were high. Yet, we have also to set this against the fact that those occupying the most disadvantaged positions display the lowest satisfaction with life, tend to be the least optimistic and have the poorest mental health (see Chapter 5). This was the cost of exposing young people to the operation of unfettered market forces.

Given these radical changes in the structure of the labour market, one would expect to have witnessed significant changes in social policy, but this was not the case in the United Kingdom. Following the Second World War, the 'problem' of youth employment was tackled by attempts to improve the apprenticeship system and, later, by making training programmes and job creation schemes available for young people. The assumption was that the state had a responsibility to help youth transition to work, so the problem for policy makers was to ensure adequate training and, if necessary, to create jobs. This approach still coloured the approach of the Labour Party, as when the recession came in the 1970s, the initial response of the Labour government was to provide jobs through a Job Creation Programme and, later, the Youth Opportunities Programme. Then, with the advent of the Conservative administration, the policy approach took a radical shift. The political elite and the business groups associated with them propounded an alternative belief that the working of the economy should be left to the operation of market forces, a belief derived from neo-classical economics in the power of the market. Government action should therefore refrain from interfering with the workings of the market. It followed that individuals were responsible for finding jobs and acquiring the skills that the market required. Policy was therefore to be limited to helping individuals to acquire the skills or human capital required by the market. The problem of unemployment came to be seen as one caused by the failure of young people to equip themselves adequately for the labour market – they had to be helped to help themselves. This led to a two-pronged approach to the youth problem.

First, it meant that the state should only provide training programmes for youth to rectify the deficiencies in their personal qualities. Second, because obtaining work was the responsibility of the young people themselves, then a series of policy measures were instigated to withdraw any form of financial support for young people to ensure that they took any jobs that were available, referred to by the authors as the 'punitive turn' of social policy. The ensuing training programmes – the Youth Opportunities Programme, the Youth Training Scheme, Modern Apprenticeship Programme and Modern Apprenticeships – were characterised by a series of common features. They were designed by civil servants without consulting employers or worker representatives, and they were centrally controlled with the sole aim of ensuring that young people acquired the skills necessary for work. They usually consisted of workplace experience, often with little or no formal training, and were often delivered through intermediaries, such as private training agencies. Trainees were provided with an income, so their services were free or heavily subsidised for the employer. They were then 'sold' to employers, in that the state also provided a financial incentive for the employer to take on the young person. At the end of the scheme, there was no guarantee of employment. In reality, these were usually workplaces at the lower end of the market, which had very short learning times and offered little more than work experience of very variable quality, as is documented in Chapters 4 and 5.

The second prong was to change the welfare system. To ensure participation in these schemes, the government gradually withdrew financial support for those who would not enter them. Starting in 1982, the government reduced welfare benefits which were later withdrawn altogether, creating a new social category of young people not in education or training (NEETs), for whom the state had no record.

What we have witnessed in the United Kingdom is a policy of blaming the victim – one that had its origins in the social and economic conditions of the 1970s, but one that has continued under the very different conditions of a globalised economy, and that, as this volume documents, entails serious costs for the young people at the bottom of the labour market. What have we learnt from other societies is that the policy response of the UK political elite is not the only possible response; in other countries, political elites have different values and beliefs and have created different institutional arrangements which have constrained the forces of globalisation and thereby mitigated the consequences for young people.

## Germany

In Germany, the impact of these global forces was modified by the country's continued adherence to the 'social partnership' approach, one characterised by labour market issues being determined through negotiations between strong employers' associations, trade unions and the state. The German political elite did not 'buy in' to the neo-classical free market ideology to the same extent as the United Kingdom and did not lead such an assault on trade unions, and they maintained the institutional arrangements that functioned to shelter young people from the worst effects of the market. As a result, the forces of globalisation were present, but their impact was mediated by the German unions' ability to safeguard the security of jobs, especially in the manufacturing sector. In the service sector where the unions were weaker this was less the case, and there, flexible employment policies were more widespread and employment more insecure (Hassel 2014).

Traditionally, Germany had an extensive apprenticeship system, shaped by the employers and unions which delivered a combination of high-level college- and work-based learning, governed by a national curriculum with learning in the workplace supervised by trained meisters. This delivered highly regarded training to three-quarters of the school leavers (Thelen 2014). In the face of change, national agreements between employers and unions gave way to plant-level agreements, while in the manufacturing sector the core workforce accepted lower pay and some flexibility in return for greater security (Hassel 2014). In this context, the basic structure of the apprenticeship remained. However, as the manufacturing sector shrank and the service sector grew, the apprenticeships became increasingly differentiated between the high-end apprenticeships that ensured access to well-paid, high-skilled jobs in manufacturing and the professions and the apprenticeships leading to the increasing number of low-paid, low-skilled jobs in the service sector, where unions were traditionally weaker. Here, the pay was only slightly higher than that for the unskilled, providing little incentive for school leavers to enter them.

In the traditional apprenticeships system, there had always been a small group (up to 10 per cent) who were unsuccessful in obtaining an apprenticeship or who dropped out. As this group grew in size with the growth of the service sector, the government responded by introducing a state-financed 'transition system' to provide a patchwork of different opportunities for young people waiting to enter a 'real' apprenticeship. These places did not lead to vocational certification and were filled by those who only had the lowest school-leaving certificate or who had failed to secure any qualification, together with those from 'migration backgrounds'. By the mid-2000s, there were nearly as many in the transition system as in the 'real system' (Thelen and Busemeyer 2012; Thelen 2014). Together, the apprenticeship system and transition system provided a shelter for those leaving school in the recession. In addition, the government also reduced the employee and employer unemployment insurance contributions, subsidised short-time working and increased staffing in the public employment service and provided funding for training. The result was that during the Great Recession, when youth unemployment soared elsewhere, in Germany the youth unemployment rate actually fell, from 13.5 per cent in 2005–7 to 10.4 per cent in 2008 and 11.0 per cent in 2009 (Bell and Blanchflower 2011: 246).

## Denmark

In Denmark, the 'social partnership' took a different form. There, employers, unions and local authorities worked together to regulate both work conditions and pay, but their collaboration also extended to the formation and implementation of labour market policy, through tripartite bodies at both national and regional levels. The result has been the creation of a system of 'flexicurity' that provides employers with the flexibility in hiring and firing but a strong system of social security and active labour market policies that created security for employees. This security took the form of financial support and training opportunities and served to mitigate the adverse consequences of unemployment. It created a more comprehensive system than that found in Germany, encompassing both the manufacturing and service sectors; for example, during the Great Recession when 18 per cent of households throughout Europe confronted real economic hardship, the figure in Denmark was only 8 per cent (Madsen 2015). The same system also contained the impact of the forces of globalisation on the patterns of inequality with the Danish labour market that is characterised by low levels of segmentation, enabling workers to move between jobs of different skill levels. In addition, cooperation between employers and unions, together with high levels of trust between them, led to the creation of jobs of higher quality in terms of employee participation in decision-making and skill development (Gallie 2011).

For young people, this collaboration between the social partners created a comprehensive dual training system, combining work experience and college-based education, together with a system of regulated traineeships. In addition, the political elite have accepted that with the decline in the use of unskilled labour there is a need for young people to upskill, and this shapes their response to supporting the transition. Thus, the use of an active labour market policy has produced a de facto youth guarantee for unemployed young people. After a short spell of unemployment, they have to take part in government programmes; otherwise they lose financial support. If they do not already have a vocational education, they will be directed towards one (Madsen 2015). Thus, while young people in Denmark experienced relatively low unemployment rates during the global recession, similar to those in Germany (Bell and Blanchflower 2011: 246), the young people employed in the service sector experienced less insecurity and higher-quality training.

## Conclusion

Neither the German or Danish systems are perfect. In Germany, high levels of insecurity and low pay are found in the service sector, where young people experience lower-quality training. In Denmark, migrants tend to be excluded from the system, but there are low levels of NEETs. Each 'system' has its own intended and unintended consequences for young people. However, they illustrate that the continuity of high levels of marginality that have characterised the fate of young people documented in this book is not an inevitable consequence of the workings of the market. Rather, it is the consequence of a political reliance on the unfettered use of market forces to organise the labour market and a fossilised ideology that perceives the costs of such a system in terms of the constant movement between low-skilled, part-time, temporary jobs, low-quality government programmes and spells of unemployment as the responsibility of the young people condemned to enter the lower levels of the labour market. This is perpetuated by UK government policy that continues to re-cycle old ideas about how government programmes are organised, re-invent the wheel and re-brand old approaches. To address this problem, we need to unlock policy thinking from the constraints imposed upon by the neo-classical paradigm, which has long outlived its usefulness in the current context, and develop policies, based on broader humanitarian values, that are more appropriate for the next phase of economic and social development.

David N. Ashton
University of Leicester

# Appendix

## Research context

This book has its origins in the research project *The Making of the 'Precariat':
Unemployment, Insecurity and Work-Poor Young Adults in Harsh Economic
Conditions* (ESRC ES/K003755/1) that was funded via wave 1 of the Secondary
Data Analysis Initiative (SDAI) of the Economic and Social Research Council
(ESRC). The particular conditions of this initiative sought to prioritise the analysis of existing data resources, data that had already been created through past
research funded by the ESRC itself, governments or other bodies. The scheme
resonated directly with the previous work of Furlong (see, for example, Furlong
1993) and Goodwin and O'Connor (2015), where data re-use, secondary analysis
and the repurposing of existing data were central to the analyses being offered.
Regarding our own analytical and epistemological proclivities, the SDAI appealed
to us directly for a number of reasons. First, as we have argued elsewhere (see
O'Connor and Goodwin 2013), for us the secondary analysis and re-use of existing
and/or legacy data is undergirded with an ethical imperative for social researchers
to make full use of data previously collected. As we have argued,

> In these times of reduced social science research funding, is it good, ethically
> sound research practice to continue to create unique one-off cross-sectional
> studies, when data already exists on young people – respondents about which
> we already know so much? Indeed, should not more use be made of the exist-
> ing data already collected on youth to avoid intrusion and duplication?
>
> (O'Connor and Goodwin 2013: 204)

Where data already exist, where information in already known and where research
and respondents have already invested heavily in the co-creation of data, as social
scientists we are duty bound to make the best and fullest use of that data.

Second, despite the apparent 'age' of some archived data, existing data retain
significant analytical potential and can be re-considered via a more 'contemporary

conceptual lens'. Put simply, when previous researchers have collected data they have done so with their own analytical and theoretical concerns at the very heart of the data collection process. This means that they would inevitably prioritise certain themes, emphasise particular correlations or highlight particular findings key to their analytical narratives. Such analysis would also usually be offered in line with the dominant intellectual trends and discourses of that time. For example, in the analysis of classic school-to-work transitions studies, past scholars would prioritise structural determinants of school-to-work transitions, according to dominant class narratives, rather than explore the individual complexities of the transition process itself (see Goodwin and O'Connor 2005). Likewise, the practice of conceptualising labour market positions as a dichotomy between employment and unemployment, reflecting traditional, hegemonic notions of work rather than exploring the complex, ever-changing sites of youth employment or the 'shades of grey' (neither employed or unemployed) roles increasingly occupied by young people. Revisiting past and existing datasets, with different analytical concerns to the originators of the data, affords us an opportunity to develop different insights not previously considered and to develop a greater understanding *without* the need to return to the field to collect new data.

Third, we have been variously associated, as students, colleagues and co-researchers, with the some of the originators of past classic school-to-work transition studies and, as such, the opportunity to revisit some of this data as part of the project was an opportunity too good to miss. It was a chance to revisit some of the intellectual antecedents of our own approaches to understanding school-to-work transitions and would enable us to re-examine some of our own assumptions around, and understandings of, these past studies.

## The making of the 'precariat'

In responding to the SDAI call, we developed an innovative programme of research that combined an important contemporary dataset, *Understanding Society*, with two 'historical' or legacy datasets from the 1980s, exploring both the contemporary and legacy data with the same research questions. The overall objective was to undertake a secondary analysis of this contemporary and legacy data to answer the research question, '*In what ways have the experiences of unemployed, insecure and vulnerable 18–25-year-olds changed between two key periods of economic instability in the UK?*' In answering this question, we also aimed to

i   Map the nature and extent of unemployment and precarious or fragmented forms of working in the 1980s and *c.* 2010.
ii  Compare the distribution of various groups of young people between different components of the precarious zone in the 1980s and *c.* 2010.

iii   Develop an understanding of the ways in which positive and negative outcomes occur and are influenced by policy interventions occurring in both time periods.

In so doing, we hoped to gain a better understanding of the early labour market experiences of young people in difficult economic circumstances and help pave the way for more effective policies in the future. However, it is important to note that in terms of research design, only the secondary analysis of existing data would enable us to answer these questions we had set. We could have committed to undertake new field research and interviewed those who entered work, further education (FE) or the various youth training schemes that existed in the 1980s, but in so doing we would have had to rely heavily on the individual respondents' abilities to recall and reconstruct their experiences from over 30 years ago. Having access to school-to-work data, contemporaneous with the timeframe of concern, offered a level of analytical potential and accuracy (or so we hoped) that could not be achieved via a new retrospective focused cross sectional study. We used three datasets for the analysis:

(i) *Young Adults in the Labour Market* (Legacy data). The first study, partial data from which was archived in the UK Data Archive (reference UKDA Study 2664), is the *Young Adults in the Labour Market* (YA) from 1983. This research was led by Professor David Ashton and involved face-to-face, semi-structured interviews with a sample 18- to 25-year-olds carried out in four contrasting labour markets in 1982–3. The four areas, Leicester, Sunderland, St Albans and Stafford, were selected to represent a range of employment conditions (see Ashton *et al.* 1982; 1986) and resulted in an achieved sample of 1,786 young people.

> Three of the local labour markets were to be Leicester, Sunderland and St Albans, due to their contrasting industrial and occupational structures and levels of unemployment, and the knowledge the researchers had of these areas through their earlier work. The fourth locality (Stafford) had to be a readily identifiable local labour market with a high proportion of white collar workers.
> (Ashton *et al.* 1982: 13)

(ii) *Changing Structure of Youth Labour Markets* (Legacy data). The second study is the *Changing Structure of Youth Labour Markets* (CSYLM) study. This was led by Professor Ken Roberts and involved face-to-face, semi-structured interviews with 854 individuals aged 17–18 in 1985 in three contrasting labour markets: Liverpool, Walsall and Chelmsford (see Roberts *et al.* 1986).

> The aim of this research was to assess the interactive effects of changes in demand and supply, plus state interventions, for the operation of Britain's youth

labour markets in the 1980s. The fieldwork was conducted in Chelmsford, Liverpool and Walsall. These areas were deliberately selected for insights in to the main variations behind the national picture.

(Roberts *et al.* 1986: 1)

Both of the legacy projects were funded by the Department of Employment in the early 1980s and the results published initially in the Department for Employment Research Paper series (paper numbers 55 and 59, respectively). As such, these studies correspond to the last major recession, during which youth unemployment reached levels unseen since the 1930s. Both of these studies covered severely depressed labour markets (e.g. Liverpool and Sunderland) as well as areas that remained fairly buoyant (e.g. St Albans and Chelmsford) during the broader economic decline of the 1980s. Both studies focused on young people with limited post-compulsory educational experiences (YA excluded those in full-time education post-18 and those with degrees, CSYLM focused on minimum-aged school leavers). Neither the YA nor the CSYLM studies have been subject to secondary analysis since the data were collected in the mid-1980s. For example, a review of the records relating to YA from the *UK Data Service* reveals that data from this study have not been used since Ashton deposited them in the mid-1980s, nor are there any subsequent publications listed as using this data beyond those written by the original research team. Although some of the data from this research were archived, all of the original interview schedules, including detailed job summary sheets for each respondent, were archived in a storage room at University of Leicester's Centre for Labour Market Studies. These remained largely undisturbed for over 30 years. The data from the CSYLM study were never deposited in the UK Data Archive but were instead donated to, and also came to be housed at, the Centre for Labour Market Studies. They was originally donated to a researcher in the centre with the intention of the data being used for a PhD project. Although they were not used for that purpose, this inadvertently, but fortuitously for us, meant that all the original interview schedules were retained – something quite unusual in contemporary research practice.

(iii) *Understanding Society* **(Contemporary data)**. The contemporary dataset to be used is *Understanding Society*, the enhanced replacement to the British Household Panel Survey. Described as 'the largest single investment in academic social research resources ever launched in the UK', *Understanding Society* follows approximately 100,000 individuals in 40,000 households on an annual basis. In this study, we draw on waves 1 and 2, filtered to include only those individuals in the age range 18–25 (up to 6,500 individuals in wave 1, in excess of 3,000 in wave 2). These individuals, who were interviewed in 2009–10 (wave 1) and 2010–11 (wave 2), were asked a variety of questions relating to educational experiences and patterns of labour market engagement as well as covering subjective aspects of experiences in education and the labour market and plans for the future. The datasets contain detailed information on home circumstances and parental position and there are linkages to administrative data for school attainment. While designed as a longitudinal study, our analysis plans were largely confined to cross-sectional analysis, with the two waves being used in order to be able to draw on a broader range of questions (some questions are not asked in both waves). However, some longitudinal analysis was necessary to explore routes out of precarious positions.

## Analytical approach

As outlined in the previous section, the legacy studies focused on specific local labour markets, while *Understanding Society* offers data relating to a national sample. However, it was never our intention, via the secondary analysis, to use the regional data from the legacy studies as a 'proxy' for the national situation in the 1980s. Nor was it ever our intention to draw out specific regions from the Understanding Society data for direct comparison with the historic data. Indeed, the numbers would not sustain this level of analysis in any meaningful way. Instead, we focused on *typologies* of employment. In both the CSYLM study and YA study datasets, the areas covered by the survey were selected to represent labour market typologies; as highlighted already, Ashton indicated in his report that the labour markets were deliberately chosen to represent different local labour market conditions. At a broad level, these labour markets could be categorised as chronically depressed, declining, economically stable or prosperous, and our initial analysis took these typologies as a starting points. To be clear, even if we had access to a contemporary dataset that provided good coverage of the same towns as those used by Ashton and Roberts, this was not an approach we wanted to take. As such, our approach in analysing Understanding Society was to construct the same typologies: typologies that could be constructed using a number of areas that meet the core criteria. In this way, we were able to utilise the numerical power of a national dataset without sacrificing sections of the country and losing the power of the data. For example, the legacy studies offer a combined workable sample of 2,640 individuals. Filtering those individuals in the age range 18–25 from *Understanding Society* gives us 9,500 individuals from waves 1 and 2. This provided a significant amount of data to achieve our stated research aims of capturing the changes in this landscape of precarious working and highlighting the experiences of young people contained within it in two periods of instability.

The types of questions asked in the CSYLM and YA studies broadly mirrored the questions asked in *Understanding Society*. This facilitated the exploration of key themes around precarity and the labour market experiences of young people in two key periods of labour market and economic instability. Illustrative themes can be summarised as

| 'Legacy' datasets | Understanding Society |
|---|---|
| **Personal and family characteristics:** age at interview, gender, ethnicity, domestic circumstances, parental occupation and education, receipt of statebenefits, income | **Personal and family characteristics:** age at interview, gender, ethnicity, domestic circumstances parental occupations and education, receipt of state benefits (jobseeker, incapacity, tax credits), income |
| **Education:** age at leaving school; highest qualification, qualifications obtained, post-school education; attitude to school/leaving, intentions and experiences of FE/higher education (HE) | **Education:** age at leaving school, highest qualification, vocational qualification, qualifications obtained, intentions and experiences of FE/HE |
| **Employment:** employment history, occupational aspirations, jobs held, hours worked and overtime, SOC for first job and current job, occupation at first and current job, permanent/temporary, self-employment, job tasks, size of organisation, job satisfaction, managerial/supervisory roles | **Employment:** employment history, jobs held (length of time), hours worked and overtime, SOC for first job and current job, occupation at first and current job, permanent/ temporary, self-employment, job tasks, size of organisation, job satisfaction, managerial/supervisory roles |
| **Unemployment:** periods of unemployment, reasons for unemployment, benefits and support, job seeking behaviour and method, problems encountered | **Unemployment:** periods of unemployment, reasons for unemployment, job seeking behaviour and methods, experience of discrimination |
| **Training:** access to training attitudes to training, types of training received, number of training periods, training providers | **Training:** access to training, discrimination in access to training, vocational qualifications, training providers |
| **Precarious work forms:** full-time/ part-time, non-standard working, pay and rewards, pensions, trade union membership, job stability, fixed-term employment, agency work, casual employment, low working hours, participation in government schemes, degree of autonomy, responsibility for others, engaging work | **Precarious work forms:** job security, full-time/part-time, non-standard working, pay and rewards, pensions, fixed-term employment, agency work, seasonal and casual employment, low working hours, participation in government schemes, degree of autonomy, responsibility for others, engaging work, receipt of state benefits |

## Legacy study data 're-use': Practical issues and concerns

### *'Practical' concerns*

In the previous section we outlined the broader intellectual case for secondary analysis and data re-use. However, while these broad aims are what we 'aspired' to, there is a 'lived reality', both practical and analytic, in repurposing data from legacy research projects. We have offered a fuller discussion of this elsewhere (see, for example, Hadfield *et al.* 2015), but it is useful here, and instructional to others, to review three areas of concern – these were organisational, definitional and interpretational issues. First, organisational issues. The interview schedules from the legacy projects had been stored in cardboard packing boxes for 30 years in a secure 'outhouse'. While the interview booklets were largely in good order, save for the occasional spotting of damp or mould, the schedules were jumbled up and, in some cases, the job summary forms had become detached. Some of the packing boxes also contained interview schedules from both the CSYLM and YA studies. As such, we began the large undertaking of reassembling the interview schedules, arranging them by project and sorting them by sequence number or unique identification number derived from the administrative data inside the questionnaire. These were then sorted into the relevant local labour market. Identifying the questionnaires by research study for the majority could be done on appearance, as one of the studies had a distinct booklet design. Once this process was complete, the data were entered into a bespoke database built in FileMaker Pro dataset. While this all may seem like 'humdrum administrative' research, it is important to note the organisation issues for two reasons. First, it took a considerable amount of time to organise the data, indeed far more time than we had expected. Second, without committing time to organising the booklets, sorting the schedules and entering the data into a database, we would not have had such an immense data resource.

Second, definitional issues. The interviews were undertaken during the early to mid-1980s and so, inevitably, the schedules contained definitions and general terminology specific to work and employment and to the youth labour markets of that time. Furthermore, the interview schedules included specific social, political and cultural references that would make little sense to anyone born post-1986. For example, it is relatively easy to find a definition for YTS (Youth Training Scheme) but what is much more complex is that YTS is used to describe a scheme that had multiple variations and pathways throughout. Without extensive scouring of past texts and policy literature, it would have been impossible to define appropriately some of the key terms used in the research. However, more problematic were the words used that no longer reflect acceptable research practice or the use of racist or sexist terminology. Although relatively rare in the data, reading respondents being defined by those in the field as 'coloured' was both troubling and analytically problematic, given that such a meaningless term obscures the ethnic identity of the respondent totally.

Finally, interpretational issues. Although we have all of the original interview schedules relating to both the CSYLM and YA studies, in the case of the CSYLM we did not have a codebook or data dictionary. For YA, we had the data dictionary for the archived component of the dataset, but we did not have any materials to help decode the employment component sheets that had not been archived previously. It was clear in both studies that a combination of fieldworkers, the research team and those doing the analysis had already annotated the schedules and applied specific codes to responses and outcomes. We could transcribe the 'raw data', but we also needed 'decode' the already coded data (Hadfield *et al.* 2015). For example, using the YA study employment component sheets to illustrate the issues we encountered, while codes such as 'j1', 'j2' may be relatively easy to interpret in the context of an employment study (job 1, job 2 and so on), other codes, such as 'LH', 'C', 'CH' and 'M', among other handwritten annotations, were less than transparent. The only way we could resolve these ambiguities with any sense of certainty was to interview members of the original research teams so that we may 'recreate' the codes from memory. However, even this was less than straightforward as there are multiple instances in the legacy studies where multiple and different codes, applied by different creators/users of the data, are applied to the same question and response.

### Race and ethnicity in the 1980s datasets

Neither of the 1980s projects focused attention on race and ethnicity as a key variable in understanding youth employment in the 1980s. This is, in part, a reflection of sociological practice in the early 1980s, although it is important to note that in both studies there was an awareness of the potential danger of omitting such a key variable from the research design.

In the case of Ashton *et al.* (1986), a note is included in the report to explain how and why ethnicity was excluded from the study. They note that of the labour markets included in the research, Leicester was known to have a demographic profile that included a high percentage of young people from minority ethnic backgrounds. To account for this, the researchers explained that they

> agreed that those districts with known high concentrations of ethnic minority groups, predominantly in the inner city, were to be avoided. It was felt that their inclusion would given an unnecessary bias to the sample for a project which was not focussing on race or ethnicity as central issues.
>
> (Ashton *et al.* 1986: 13)

This is not to say that during the early 1980s the experience of black and Asian youth in the city was being ignored. A number of studies were carried out that focused exclusively on transition from school to work of minority ethnic young people in the city (e.g. Brah and Golding 1983), but there was little evidence of ethnicity being mainstreamed.

In common with Ashton *et al.* (1986), Roberts *et al.* (1987: 137) did not include 'acceptable and meaningful questions' on ethnicity as part of their project.

However, they did identify that their sample included a small number of black and Asian young people in two of the selected labour markets (Liverpool and Walsall), and they provided some limited analysis of the data they had. They contrasted the experience of the small number of minority ethnic young people with the wider sample and acknowledged that the differences that emerge were of interest and certainly worthy of greater attention, suggesting, for example, that the impact of discrimination on the minority ethnic youth in their sample would likely increase 'as the young people move from relatively sheltered educational environments into the labour market'. However, given the small sample size, little attention is paid to this issue in the main study.

We are conscious that the data we have been able to access from the legacy studies did not account for race and ethnicity as a significant variable, and this omission conflicts with current practice. However, with so little data on race and ethnicity from the 1980s available to us, we have not used this as a variable used for analysis. This is a limitation of the study that we acknowledge.

# Bibliography

Abrams, M. (1959) *The teenage consumer*. London, Press Exchange

Ashton, D. (1986) *Unemployment under capitalism: The sociology of British and American labour markets*. Brighton: Harvester Press.

Ashton, D. N. (2017, forthcoming) Globalisation and its impact on the political, economic and labour markets aspects of the transition, in *Young people's development and the Great Recession: Uncertain transitions and precarious futures*. Cambridge: Cambridge University Press.

Ashton, D. N. and Field, D. (1976) *Young workers: From school to work*. London: Hutchinson.

Ashton, D. N., Maguire, M. J. and Garland, V. (1982) *Youth in the labour market*. London: Department of Employment.

Ashton, D. N., Maguire, M. J., Bowden, D., Dellow, P., Kennedy, S., Stanley, G., Woodhead, G. and Jennings, B. (1986) *Young adults in the labour market*. London: Department of Employment.

Ashton, D., Maguire, M. and Spilsbury, M. (1990) *Restructuring the labour market: The implications for youth*. London: Macmillan.

Atkinson, A. B. (2015) *Inequality: What can be done?* London: Harvard University Press.

Atkinson, A. B., Piketty, T. and Saez, E. (2011) Top incomes in the long run of history. *Journal of Economic Literature*, 49 (1): 3–71.

Ball, S. (2013) *Foucault, power and education*. London: Routledge.

Banks, M. H. and Ullah, P. (1988) *Youth unemployment in the 1980s: Its psychological effects*. London: Croom Helm.

Baum, A., Ma, J. and Payea, K. (2013) *Education pays: The benefits of higher education for individuals and society*. Washington: College Board.

Bauman, Z. (2000) *Liquid modernity*. Cambridge: Polity

Baur, N., and Ernst, S. (2011). Towards a process-oriented methodology: modern social science research methods and Norbert Elias's figurational sociology. In N. Gabriel and S. Mennell (eds), *Norbert Elias and figurational research: Processual Thinking in Sociology*. Malden: Wiley-Blackwell.

BBC (2011) More graduates taking low skill jobs. 12 May.

Beck, U. (1992) *Risk society: Towards a new modernity*. London: Sage.

Beck, U. (2000) *The brave new world of work*. Cambridge: Polity.

Bell, D. N. F. and Blanchflower, D. G. (2009) Youth unemployment: Déjà vu? Working paper, Stirling Management School, University of Stirling.

Bell, D. N. F. and Blanchflower, D. G. (2011) Young people and the Great Recession. *Oxford Review of Economic Policy*, 27 (2): 241–267

Bell, D. N. F. and Blanchflower, D. G. (2013) *How to measure underemployment.* Working paper 13–7. Washington: Pearson Institute for International Economics.

Bell, R. and Jones, G. (2002) *Youth policies in the UK: A chronological map*, 2nd edition. York: Funded by the Joseph Rowntree Foundation.

Benn, T, (1990) *Confidence in Her Majesty's government.* House of Commons Deb 22 November (181): cc 439–518.

Berger, M. C. (1989) Demographic cycles, cohort size and earnings. *Demography*, 26 (2): 311–321.

Berger, S. (2006) *How we compete. What companies around the world are doing to make it in today's global economy.* New York: Doubleday.

Birchall, M. (2009) Graduate jobs crisis is only going to get worse. The *Times*, 21 October: 61.

Bivand, P., Gardiner, L., Whitehurst, D. and Wilson, T. (2011) *Youth unemployment: A million reasons to act?* London: Centre for Economic and Social Inclusion.

Boffey, D. (2012) David Cameron's back-to-work firms want benefits cut more often. The *Guardian*, 30 June. Available online at www.theguardian.com/society/2012/jun/30/david-cameron-work-firms-benefits (accessed 26 November 2014).

Boland, T. and Griffin, R. (2015) The death of unemployment and the birth of job-seeking in welfare policy: Governing a liminal experience. *Irish Journal of Sociology*, 23: 29–48.

Bourdieu, P. (1977) Cultural reproduction and social reproduction, in Karabel, J. and Halsey, A. H. (eds) *Power and ideology in education.* New York: Oxford University Press.

Bourdieu, P. (2002) *Masculine Domination.* Stanford: Stanford University Press.

Boycott Workfare. Available online at http://www.boycottworkfare.org/?page_id=31.

Bradley, H. (2005) Winners and losers: Young people in the 'New Economy', in Bradley, H. and van Hoof, J. (eds) *Young People in Europe: Labour Markets and Citizenship.* Bristol: Policy Press.

Braverman, H. (1974) *Labor and monopoly capital.* New York: Free Press.

Brooks, R. and Everett, G. (2009) Post-graduation reflections on the value of a degree. *British Educational Research Journal*, 35 (3): 333–349.

Brown, P. (1987) *Schooling ordinary kids: Inequality, unemployment, and the new vocationalism.* Londin: Tavistock.

Brown, P. and Hesketh, A. (2004) *The mismanagement of talent: Employability and jobs in the knowledge economy.* Oxford: Oxford University Press.

Brown, P., Hesketh, A. and Williams, S. (2003) Employability in a knowledge-driven economy. *Journal of Education and Work*, 16 (2): 107–126

Brown, P., Lauder, H. and Ashton, D. (2011) *The global auction. The broken promises of education, jobs and incomes.* New York: Oxford.

Butler, P. and Malik, S. (2015) One in six jobseekers have allowances stopped by DWP each year. The *Guardian*, 5 August. Available online at https://www.theguardian.com/society/2015/aug/05/jobseekers-dole-guardian-research-government-welfare.

Byrnin, M. (2013) Individual choice and risk: The case of higher education. *Sociology*, 47 (2): 284–300.

Campbell, I. (2015) Youth unemployment 'crisis' more about job quality. *The Conversation*, 1 October.

Carter, M. P. (1962) *Home, school and work*. Oxford: Pergamon.

Castel, R. (2003) *From manual workers to wage laborers: Transformation of the social question*. Brunswick, NJ: Transaction.

CBI (2009) *Employment trends 2009*. London: CBI.

Chamberlin, G. (2010) Output and expenditure in the last three UK recessions. *Economic & Labour Market Review*, 4 (8): 51–64.

Clark, A. (1993) *Diaries: In power 1983–1992*. London: Phoenix.

Clarke, J. and Willis, P. (1984) Introduction, in Bates, I., Clarke, J., Cohen, P., Finn, D., Moore, R. and Willis, P. *Schooling for the dole? The new vocationalism*. Basingstoke: Macmillan.

Clark, T. and Heath, A. (2014) *Hard times. The divisive toll of the economic slump*. London: Yale University Press.

Clement, M. (2015) Thatcher's civilising offence: The Ridley Plan to decivilise the working class. *Human Figurations*, 4 (1): n.p.

Cockburn, C. (1987) *Two-track training: Sex inequalities and the YTS*. London: Macmillan Education.

Comfort, N. (2012) *The slow death of British industry: A 60-year suicide, 1952–2012*. London: Biteback.

Conservative Party (1979) Conservative Party Manifesto 1979. Available online at www. conservativemanifesto.com.

Ćorić, B. (2011) The sources of the Great Moderation: A survey. Challenges of Europe: Growth & Competitiveness – Reversing the Trends. Ninth International Conference Proceedings. 26–28 May, Split, Croatia, pp. 185–205.

Craig, R. (2007) *Business Law*, 8th edition. London: Cengage Learning.

Crisp, R. and POWELL, R. (2016) Young people and UK labour market policy: a critique of 'employability' as a tool for understanding youth unemployment. *Urban Studies*, 54 (8): 1784–1807.

Davies, B. (1982) What most young people really want is a job. The *Guardian*, 10 August.

Deakin, B.M. (1996) *The youth labour market in Britain: The role of intervention*. Cambridge: Cambridge University Press.

Dolton, P., Galinda-Rueda, F. and Makepeace, G. (2004) *The long term effects of government sponsored training*. Available online at http://webarchive.nationalarchives.gov. uk/20130401151715/http://www.education.gov.uk/publications/eOrderingDownload/ RW18.pdf.

Douglas, J. W. B. (1967) *The home and the school: A study of ability and attainment in the primary school*. St Albans: Panther.

Douglas, M. (1966) *Purity and danger: An analysis of concepts of pollution and taboo*. London: Routledge Kegan Paul.

Du Bois Reymond, M. and Plug, W. (2005) Young people and their contemporary labour market values, in Bradley, H. and van Hoof, J. (eds) *Young people in Europe: Labour markets and citizenship*. Bristol: Policy Press.

Duckworth, K. and Schoon, I. (2012) Beating the odds: Exploring the impact of social risk on young people's school to work transition during recession in the UK. *National Institute Economic Review*, 222: R38-R49.

Dunning, E. and Hughes, J. (2013) *Norbert Elias and modern sociology: Knowledge, interdependence, power, process*. London: Bloomsbury Academic.

Eckersley, R. (2009) Progress, culture and young people's wellbeing, in Furlong, A. (ed.) *Handbook of youth and young adulthood*. London: Routledge.

Edwards, D. S. (1985) The History and politics of the Youth Opportunities Programme 1978–1983. PhD thesis submitted to the University of London Institute for Education.

Elias, N. (1961) *Application for a grant for special research to DSIR*. Unpublished manuscript (Teresa Keil Collection), University of Leicester, UK.

Elias, N. (1962) *Second memorandum, unpublished*. Marbach: Deutsches Literaturarchiv.

Elias, N. (1987) Retreat of the sociologists, *Theory, Culture and Society* 4(2): 223–247.

Elias, N. (1994) *Reflections on a life*. London: Polity.

Elias, N. (2000) *The Civilising process*. London: Blackwell.

Elias, N. (2001) *The Society of individuals*. London: Blackwell.

Elias, N. (2006) 'Über den rückzug der soziologen auf die gegenwart', in *Aufsätze undandere Schriften II*, Gesammelte Schriften, Vol. 15. Frankfurt am Main: Suhrkamp: 389–408

Elias, N. (2010) *The society of individuals*, Collected Works Edition, Vol. 10. Dublin: University College Dublin Press.

Elias, N. (2012) On the process of civilisation: Sociogenetic and psychogenetic investigations. *The Collected Works of Norbert Elias*, Vol. 3. Dublin: University College Dublin Press.

Emmenegger, P., Häusermann, S., Palier, B. and Seeleib-Kaiser, M. (2012) *The age of dualization: The changing face of inequality in deindustrializing societies*. Oxford: Oxford University Press.

Evans, J. (1985) Contribution to youth training scheme debate. House of Commons. Hansard, Deb 01 July 1985 vol 82 cc24–33.

Fairley, J. (1982) The great training robbery. *Marxism Today*, November: 28–32.

Felstead, A., Krahn, H. and Powell, M. (1997) *Contrasting fortunes across the life course: Non-standard work among women and men in Canada and the United Kingdom*, CLMS Working Paper No. 17, Centre for Labour Market Studies, Leicester University, May.

Fenton, S. and Dermott, E. (2006) Fragmented careers? Winners and losers in young adult labour markets. *Work, Employment and Society*, 20 (2): 205–221.

Fevre, R. (2007) Employment insecurity and social theory: The power of nightmares. *Work, Employment and Society*, 21: 517–535.

Finn, D. (1987) *Training without jobs*. London: MacMillan.

Fogelman, K. (1985) After school: The educational and training experiences of the 1958 cohort. NCDS Working Paper No. 3. London: Social Statistics Research Unit, City University.

Furlong, A. (1992) *Growing up in a classless society? School to work transitions*. Edinburgh: Edinburgh University Press.

Furlong, A. and Cartmel, F. (1997) *Young people and social change: Individualization and risk in late modernity*. Buckingham: Open University Press.

Furlong, A. and Cartmel, F. (2004) *Vulnerable young men in fragile labour markets*. York: York Publishing.

Furlong, A. and Cartmel, F. (2009) *Higher education and social justice*. Buckingham: Open University Press.

Furlong, A. and McNeish, W. (2000) Integration through training. Report to the European Commission. Glasgow: University of Glasgow.

Furlong, A. and Kelly, P. (2005) The Brazilianization of youth transitions in Australia and the UK? *Australian Journal of Social Issues*, 40 (2): 207–225.

Furlong, A., Cartmel, F., Biggart, A., Sweeting, H. and West, P. (2003) *Youth transitions: Patterns of vulnerability and processes of social exclusion*. Edinburgh: Scottish Government.

Fuller, A. and Unwin, L. (2013) *Gender segregation, apprenticeship and the raising of the participation age in England: Are young women at a disadvantage?* London: Centre for Learning and Life Chances in Knowledge Economies and Societies.

Furlong, A. and Cartmel, F. (2007) *Young people and social change: New perspectives*. London: McGraw-Hill.

Gallie, D, (2011) Production regimes, employee job control and skill development. LLAKES Research Paper 31. London Institute of Education.

Gallie, D. and Paugam, S. (2002) *Social precarity and social integration*. Brussels: European Commission.

Gallie, D., Felstead, A., Green, F. and Inanc, H. (2014) The quality of work in Britain over the economic crisis. *International Review of Sociology*, 4 (2): 207–224.

Giddens, A. (1990) *The consequences of modernity*. Oxford: Polity.

Gomez P.-Y. and Korine, H. (2008) *Entrepreneurs and democracy: A political theory of corporate governance*. Cambridge: Cambridge University Press.

Goodwin, J. (2007) The transition to work and adulthood: Becoming adults via communities of practice, in Hughes, J., Jewson, N. and Unwin, L. (2007) *Communities of practice: Critical perspectives*. London: Routledge.

Goodwin, J. and Hughes, J. (2011) Ilya Neustadt, Norbert Elias, and the development of sociology in Britain: Formal and informal sources of historical data. *British Journal of Sociology*, 26 (4): 677–695.

Goodwin, J. and O'Connor, H. (2005) Exploring complex transitions: Looking back on the 'golden age' of from school to work. *Sociology*, 39 (2): 201–220.

Goodwin, J. and O'Connor, H. (2015) *Norbert Elias's Lost Research: Revisiting the Young Worker Project*. Farnham: Ashgate.

Goos, M. and Manning, A. (2007) Lousy and lovely jobs: The rising polarization of jobs in Britain. *Review of Economics and Statistics*, 89 (1): 118–133.

Green, F. (ed.) (1989) *The restructuring of the UK economy*. Hemel Hempstead: Harvester Wheatsheaf.

Green, F. (2006) *Demanding work. The paradox of job quality in the affluent economy*. Princeton: Princeton University Press.

Green, F., Felstead, A., Gallie, D. and Inanc, H. (2014) Job-related well-being through the Great Recession. *Journal of Happiness Studies*, 18 December. Available online at http://orca.cf.ac.uk/71606/1/JOHS-D-13-00322_4threvision.pdf.

Hadfield, S., Goodwin, J., O'Connor, H. and Plugor, R. (2015) *Researching precarious work and youth labour markets: Practical and methodological issues in secondary analysis of historical data*. Sociology Occasional Paper, Department of Sociology, University of Leicester.

Hall, S., Massey, D. and Rustin, M. (2013) *After neoliberalism: The Kilburn Manifesto*. London: Soundings. Available online at www.lwbooks.co.uk/journals/soundings/manifesto.html (accessed 20 May 2015).

Hart, P.E. (1988) *Youth unemployment in Great Britain*. Cambridge: Cambridge University Press.

Hassel, A. (2014) The paradox of liberalization – Understanding dualism and the recovery of the German political economy. *British Journal of Industrial Relations*, 52 (1): 57–81.

Hochschild, A. (1983) *The managed heart*. Berkeley: University of California Press.

Holland, G. (1977) *Young people and work*. Sheffield: Manpower Services Commission.

Hollands, R. G. (1990) *The long transition: Class, culture and youth training*. Basingstoke: Macmillan.

Hughes, J., Jewson, N. and Unwin, L. (2007) Communities of practice – A contested concept in flux, in Hughes, J., Jewson, N. and Unwin, L. (2007) *Communities of practice: Critical perspectives*. London: Routledge.

Hunter, L., McGregor, A., MacInnes, J. and Sproull, A. (1993) The 'flexible firm': Strategy and segmentation. *British Journal of Industrial Relations*, 31 (3): 383–407.

*Independent*, The (1995) Youth Training Scheme a failure and a disgrace, Labour says. 13 February. Available online at www.independent.co.uk/news/youth-training-scheme-a-failure-and-a-disgrace-labour-says-1572820.html.

International Labour Office (1930) Convention Concerning Forced or Compulsory Labour. Adopted Geneva, 28 June 1930.

International Labour Office (1957) Abolition of Forced Labour Convention, Adopted Geneva, 25 June 1957.

International Labour Office (2014) Standard setting on forced labour at the 103rd Session of the International Labour Conference. Geneva, 28 May to 12 June. Available online at www. ilo.org/wcmsp5/groups/public/---ed_norm/---declaration/documents/briefingnote/wcms_243395.pdf (accessed 12 May 2015).

Jackson, B. and Marsden, D. (1962) *Education and the working class*. London: Routledge and Kegan Paul.

Jackson, M. P. (1985) *Youth unemployment*. Beckenham: Croom Helm.

Jones, P. J. (2014) *'He is(n't) one of us': Liminality and the sons-in-law in Downton Abbey*. Paper presented at the PCA/ACA National Conference 2014 Popular Culture Association/American Culture Association. Chicago, 17 April.

Jorens, Y., Gillis, D., Valcke, L. and De Coninck, J. (2015) *Atypical employment in aviation: Final report*. Brussels: European Commission.

Junankar, P. N. (1987) The labour market for young people, in Junankar, P. N. (ed.) *From school to unemployment?* London: Macmillan.

Kerckhoff, A.C. Growing up in a classless society? School to work transitions. *American Journal of Sociology*, 99 (6): 1691–1693.

Kintrea, K., St Clair, R. and Houston, M. (2015) Shaped by place? Young people's aspirations in disadvantaged neighbourhoods. *Journal of Youth Studies*, 18 (5): 666–684.

Klapcsik, S. (2012) *Liminality in fantastic fiction: A poststructuralist approach*. Jefferson: McFarland.

La Shure, C. (2005) What is liminality? 18 October. Available online at www.liminality. org/about/whatisliminality/ (accessed 13 October 2016).

Lave, J. and Wenger, E. (1991) *Situated learning: Legitimate peripheral participation.* Cambridge: Cambridge University Press.

Lee, D., Marsden, D., Hardy, M., Rickman, P. and Masters, K. (1987) Youth training, life chances and orientations to work: A case study of the Youth Training Scheme, in Brown, P. and Ashton, D. (eds) *Education, unemployment and labour markets.* London: The Falmer Press.

Lee, D., Marsden, D., Rickman, P. and Duncombe, J. (1990) *Scheming for youth: A study of YTS in the enterprise culture.* Milton Keynes: Open University Press.

Lopez-Aguado, P. (2012) Working between two worlds: Gang intervention and street liminality. *Ethnography*, 14 (2): 186–206.

MacDonald, R. (2011) Youth transitions, unemployment and underemployment: Plus ça change, plus c'est la même chose? *Journal of Sociology*, 47 (4): 427–444.

MacDonald, R. (2016) 'Precarious work: The growing precarité of youth, in Furlong, A. (ed.) *Handbook of youth and young adulthood.* London: Routledge.

MacDonald, R. and Marsh, J. (1995) *Disconnected youth: Growing up in Britain's poor neighbourhoods.* Basingstoke, Palgrave Macmillan.

MacDonald, R. and Marsh, J. (2001) Disconnected youth? *Journal of Youth Studies*, 4 (February 2015): 373–391.

MacDonald, R., Shildrick, T. and Furlong, A. (2013) In search of 'intergenerational cultures of worklessness': Hunting the Yeti and shooting zombies. *Critical Social Policy*, 26 (2): 199–220.

McDowell, L. (2003) *Redundant masculinities: Employment change and white working class youth.* Oxford: Blackwell.

MacInnes, T., Aldridge, H., Bushe, S., Kenway, P. and Tinson, A. (2013) *Monitoring poverty and social exclusion.* London: New Policy Institute.

McKie, L. (1989) *The moral economy of unemployment: Working on & participating in the Youth Training Scheme (Co. Durham 1983–1986).* Durham theses, Durham University. Available online at http://etheses.dur.ac.uk/9302/.

Maclagan, I. (1996) How successful are Modern Apprenticeships? Working brief. London: Unemployment Unit, pp. 14–16

McRobbie, A. (1989) Motherhood, a teenage job. The *Guardian*, 5 September, pp. 17.

Mack, J. and Lansley, S. (1985) *Poor Britain.* London: George Allen and Unwin.

Madsen, P. K. (2015) Youth unemployment and the skills mismatch in Denmark. Committee on Employment and Social Affairs, Policy Department and Economic and Scientific Policy, European Parliament. Available online at www.europarl.europa.eu/ RegData/etudes/IDAN/2015/536322/IPOL_IDA(2015)536322_EN.pdf.

Maguire, M. (1991) British labour market trends, in Ashton, D. and Lowe, G. (eds) *Making their way: Education, training and the labour market in Canada and Britain.* Milton Keynes: Open University Press.

Maguire, S. M. (2000) The evolving youth labour market: A study of continuity and change. PhD thesis, University of Warwick.

Mail Online (2013) It's kind of an empty cliff: Half of new graduates with bachelors degrees are unemployed or underemployed. Mail Online, 31 May.

Maizels, J. (1970) *Adolescent needs and the transition from school to work.* London: Athlone Press.

Makeham, P. (1980) *Youth unemployment.* Research Paper No. 10. London: Department of Employment.

Manyika, J., Sinclair, J., Dobbs, R., Strube, G., Rassey, L., Mischke, J., Remes, J., Roxburgh, C., George, K., O'Halloran, D. and Ramaswamy, S. (2012) *Manufacturing the future: The next era of global growth and innovation.* McKinsey Global Institute, November. Available online at www.mckinsey.com/business-functions/operations/our-insights/the-future-of-manufacturing.

Mennell, S. (2006) Civilising processes. *Theory, Culture and Society*, 23 (2–3): 429–431.

Mennell, S. (2015) Civilising offensives and decivilising processes: Between the emic and the etic. *Human Figurations*, 4 (1): n.p.

Mills, C. W. (1951) *White collar.* New York: Oxford University Press.

Mizen, P. (1990) Young people's experiences of the Youth Training Scheme: A case study of recent state intervention in the youth labour market. PhD thesis submitted to the University of Warwick.

Morgan, D. (1981) Youth-call up: Social policy for the young. *Critical Social Policy*, 1 (2): 101–110.

Mosca, I. and Wright, R. (2011) Is graduate underemployment persistent? Bonn: Institute for the Study of Labour.

Muriel, A. and Sibieta, L. (2009) *Living standards during previous recessions.* IFS Briefing Note BN85. London: Institute for Fiscal Studies.

Murray, C. (2012) Flagship work programme a 'miserable failure'. London: Reuters. Available online at http://uk.reuters.com/article/2012/11/28/uk-britain-work-idUKLNE8AQ 00M20121128 (accessed 26 November 2014).

Myck, M. (2002) How the New Deal works. *Fiscal Policy*, 19 (3): n.p.

Nilsen, A. and Brannen, J. (2014) An intergenerational approach to transitions to adulthood: The importance of history and biography. *Sociological Research Online*, 19 (2): 9.

Norbert, N. (2006), *The court society*, Collected Works, Vol. 2. Dublin: UCD Press

O'Connor, H. and Goodwin, J. (2010) Utilizing data from a lost sociological project: Experiences, insights, promises. *Qualitative Research*, 10 (3): 283–298.

O'Connor, H. and Goodwin, J. (2013) The ethical dilemmas of restudies in researching youth. *YOUNG: Nordic Journal of Youth Research*, 21 (3): 289–307.

O'Connor, H. and Bodicoat, M. (2016) Exploitation or opportunity? Student perceptions of internships in enhancing employability skills. *British Journal of Sociology of Education*, 4 January.

OECD (1980) The Impact of oil on the world economy. *OECD Economic Studies*, 27: 114–130.

OECD (2012) Labour losing to capital: What explains the declining labour share?, in *OECD employment outlook.* Paris: OECD.

Office for National Statistics (2006) Consumer price inflation: 1947–2004. *Economic Trends*, 626. London: ONS.

Office for National Statistics (2014) *Young people in the labour market.* London: ONS.

O'Higgins, N. (2001) Youth unemployment and employment policy: A global perspective. Geneva: International Labour Office.

Osgerby, B. (1998) *Youth in Britain since 1945.* London: Blackwell.

Pollett, A. (1988) The 'flexible firm': Fixation or fact? *Work, Employment and Society*, 2 (3): 282–316.

Radical History Network (2009) Claimants and unemployed issues and struggles in the 1970s and 1980s (especially Tottenham in the 1980s) – what can we learn from them? Available online at http://radicalhistorynetwork.blogspot.co.uk/2009/10/claimants-and-unemployed-issues-and.html (accessed 25 July 2014).

Raffe, D. (1981) Education, employment and the Youth Opportunities Programme: Some sociological perspectives. *Oxford Review of Education*, 7 (3): 211–222.

Raffe, D. (1986) Change and continuity in the youth labour market: A critical review of structural explanations of youth unemployment, in Allen, S., Watson, A., Purcell, K. and Woods, S. (eds) *The experience of unemployment*. London: Macmillan.

Raffe, D. and Williams, J. D. (1989) Schooling the discouraged worker: Local-labour market effects in educational participation. *Sociology*, 23 (4): 559–581.

Reuters (2013) UK economy heads for recession. Available online at http://uk.reuters.com/article/2012/01/25/uk-britain-economy-idUKTRE80N0KE20120125 (accessed 8 January 2014).

Riley, R. and Young, G. (2000) *The New Deal for young people: Implications for employment and the public finance*. London: National Institute for Economic and Social Research.

Roberts, K. (1975) The developmental theory of occupational choice: A critique and an alternative, in Esland, G., Salman, G. and Speakman, M.-A. (eds) *People and work*. Edinburgh: Holmes McDougall.

Roberts, K. (1995) *Youth and employment in modern Britain*. Oxford: Oxford University Press.

Roberts, K., Dench, S. and Richardson, D. (1986) *The changing structure of youth labour markets*. Research paper number 59. London: Department of Employment.

Roberts, S. (2010) Beyond 'NEET' and 'tidy' pathways: Considering the 'missing middle' of youth transition studies. *Journal of Youth Studies*, 14 (1): 21–39.

Roberts, S. and Evans, S. (2013) Aspirations and imagined futures: The impossibilities for Britain's young working classes. New Agendas on Youth and Young Adulthood conference. Glasgow, 8–10 April.

Roberts. S. and MacDonald, R. (2013) Introduction for special section of *Sociological Research Online*: The marginalised mainstream: Making sense of the 'missing middle' of youth studies. *Sociological Research Online*, 18 (1): 21.

Rutter, M. and Smith, D. J. (eds) (1995) *Psycho-social disorders among young people: Time trends and their causes*. Chichester: John Wiley and Sons

Ryan, P. (1989) Youth interventions, job substitution, and trade union policy in Great Britain, 1976–1986, in Rosenberg, S. (ed.) *The state and the labour market: Plenum studies in work and industry*. New York: Springer.

Ryan, P. and Unwin, L. (2001) Apprenticeship in the British 'training market'. *National Institute Economic Review*, 178: 99–114.

Sennett, R. (1998) *The corrosion of character: The personal consequences of work in the new capitalism*. New York: Norton.

Shildrick, T., MacDonald, R., Webster, C. and Gathwaite, K. (2010) *The low-pay, no-pay cycle: Understanding recurrent poverty*. York, Joseph Rowntree Foundation.

Shildrick, T., MacDonald, R., Furlong, A., Roden, J. and Crow, R. (2012) *Are 'cultures of worklessness' passed down the generations?* York: Joseph Rowntree Foundation.

Sinfield, A. (1981) *What unemployment means*. Oxford: Martin Robertson.

Sissons, P. (2011) *The hourglass and the escalator: Labour market change and mobility*. London: The Work Foundation.

Spence, A. (2011) Labour market. *Social Trends*, 41. London: Office for National Statistics.

Stafford, A. (1981) Learning not to labour, *Capital and Class*, 15 (Autumn): 55–77

Standing, G. (2011) *The Precariat: The new dangerous class*. London: Bloomsbury.

Stock, J. H. and Watson, M. W. (2002) Has the business cycle changed and why?, in Gertler, M. and Rogoff, K. (eds) *National Bureau of Economic Research Macroeconomics Annual 2002*, 17.

Stokes, H. (2012) *Imagining futures: Identity narratives and the role of work, education, community and family*. Melbourne: Melbourne University Press.

Thelen, K. (2014) *Varieties of liberalization and the new politics of social solidarity*. New York: Cambridge University Press.

Thelen, K. and Busemeyer, M. (2012) Institutional change in German vocational training: From collectivism toward segmentalism, in Busemeyer, M. and Rampusch, C. (eds) *The political economy of collective skill formation*. Oxford: Oxford University Press.

Theodore, N. and Peck, J. (2014) Selling flexibility: Temporary staffing in a volatile economy, in Fudge, J. and Strauss, K. (eds) *Temporary work, agencies and unfree labour: Insecurity in the new world of work*. London: Routledge.

Threadgold, S. (2015) Creativity, precarity and maintaining a hopeful future: DIY cultures and 'strategic poverty'. Paper presented to the Young People and Politics of Outrage and Hope conference. University of Newcastle NSW, 7–8 December.

Tomlinson, M. (2013) *Education, work and identity: Themes and perspectives*. London: Bloomsbury.

Trades Union Congress (2012) One million more people have joined under-employed workforce since 2008. 3 September. Available online at tuc.org.uk/economic-issues/economic-analysis/labour-market/one-million-more-people-have-joined-under-employed.

Trades Union Congress (2013) The UK's low pay recovery. London: TUC.

Turner, V. (1967) *The forest of symbols: Aspects of Ndembu ritual*. Ithaca: Cornell University Press.

Turner, V. (1969) *The ritual process: Structure and anti-structure*. Chicago: Aldine.

Turner, V. (1974) Liminal to liminoid, in play, flow, and ritual: An essay in comparative symbology. *Rice University Studies*, 60 (3): 53–92

Turner, V. (1980) Social dramas and stories about them. *Critical Inquiry*, 7: 141–68.

Tweedie, D. (2013) Making sense of insecurity: A defence of Richard Sennett's sociology of work. *Work, Employment and Society*, 27: 94–104.

Tyler, I. (2013) The riots of the underclass?: Stigmatisation, mediation and the government of poverty and disadvantage in neoliberal Britain. *Sociological Research Online*, 18 (4): 6.

University of Essex. (2014) Institute for Social and Economic Research, NatCen Social Research. *Understanding Society: Waves 1–6, 2009–2015*. [data collection]. 6th edition. UK Data Service. SN: 6614. Available online at http://dx.doi.org/10.5255/UKDA-SN-6614-6.

Van Gennep, A. (1909/1977) *The rites of passage*. London: Routledge and Kegan Paul.

Vickerstaff, S. (2003) Apprenticeship in the 'Golden Age': Were youth transitions really smooth and unproblematic back then? *Work, Employment and Society*, 17 (2): 269–287.

Wacquant, L. (2008) *Urban outcasts: A comparative sociology of advanced marginality*. Cambridge: Polity.

Walker, M. (1997) EU gets to work on jobs. The *Guardian*, 21 November, p. 14.

Walkerdine, V., Lucey, H. and Melody, J. (2001) *Growing up girl: Psychosocial explorations of gender and class*. London: Palgrave.

Wallace, C. (1987) *For richer, for poorer: Growing up in and out of work*. London: Tavistock.

Warr, P. (1990) The measurement of well-being and other aspects of mental health. *Journal of Occupational Psychology*, 63: 193–210.

Webb, S. and Webb, B. (1911) *The prevention of destitution*. London: Longman, Green and Co.

Wenger, E. (1998) *Communities of practice: Learning, meaning and identity*. Cambridge: Cambridge University Press.

West, M. and Newton, P. (1983) *The transition from school to work*. London: Croom Helm.

West, P. (2009) Health in youth: Changing times and changing influences, in Furlong, A. (ed.) *Handbook of youth and young adulthood*. London: Routledge.

West, P. and Sweeting, H. (1996) Nae job, nae future: Young people and health in the context of unemployment. *Health and Social Care in the Community*, 4: 50–62.

Wierenga, A. (2009) *Young people making a life*. Basingstoke: Palgrave Macmillan.

Wight, D. (1993) *Workers not wasters*. Edinburgh: Edinburgh University Press.

Willis, P. (1977) *Learning to Labour*. Farnborough: Saxon House.

Wilson, H. (1963) Labour's plan for science. Speech to the Labour Party conference, Scarborough.

Wilson, W. J. (1990) *The truly disadvantaged: The inner city, the underclass and public policy*. Chicago, University of Chicago Press.

Woodman, D. (2012) Life out of synch: How new patters of further education and the rise of precarious employment are reshaping young people's relationships. *Sociology*, 46: 1074–1090.

Youthaid (1981) *Study of the transition from school to working life: Volume II*. London: Youthaid.

Youthaid (1986) Part-time teenagers 'exploited'. *Youthaid Bulletin*, July/August. London: Youthaid.

# Index